Family Karma

Family Karma

The Hidden Ties That Bind

Kevin J. Todeschi

With Wisdom from the Edgar Cayce Readings

ARE
PRESS

**ASSOCIATION FOR
RESEARCH AND
ENLIGHTENMENT**

A.R.E. Press • Virginia Beach • Virginia

A.R.E. Press
215 67th Street
Virginia Beach, VA 23451-2061

Library of Congress Cataloguing-in-Publication Data
Todeschi, Kevin J.
  Family karma : the hidden ties that bind / by Kevin J. Todeschi
    p. cm.
  ISBN 0-87604-505-0 (trade pbk. : alk. paper)
  1. Karma. 2. Reincarnation. 3. Family–Miscellanea. 4. Cayce, Edgar, 1877-1945. I. Title.
  BF1045.K37T63 2005
  133.9—dc22

                    2005027818

Cover design by Richard Boyle

Be not deceived; God is not mocked:
for whatsoever a man soweth, that shall he also reap.
Galatians 6:7

Contents

Preface

Life is a completely lawful experience. This statement is an absolute truth regardless of our personal feelings to the contrary: Life IS a completely lawful experience.

Although no one could dispute the fact that innumerable laws govern, shape and guide our everyday lives, perhaps many would question the absolute lawfulness of life. To be sure, we have laws regarding behavior, property, driving, business, relationships, taxes, quality control, international affairs, transportation, education, personal conduct—the list goes on and on. Among these laws, we have laws that apply to everyone, such as laws against criminal activity. We also have laws that are geared to a more limited audience, such as laws prohibiting insider trading. We have laws that apply only to individual neighborhoods, such as covenant agreements, and we have laws that apply only to specific religions (such as dietary laws), cultures (such as appropriate attire and dress) or countries (such as travel and trading restrictions).

Laws are an everyday constant in our lives.

However, it is not necessarily because of human-made laws that life is completely lawful; in fact, sometimes it is actually in spite of these laws that personal lawfulness still comes into being. Life is a completely lawful experience because there is a higher law that is universal in scope and yet remains generally unknown by countless individuals the world over. It is a law that is in effect at all times, that is applicable in every circumstance, and that comes into play in every situation. It is a law that is relevant to and associated with every deed, every thought, every spoken word and every activity. This law governs all people everywhere—without exception—and it has been in existence since the dawn of Creation. This law is the law of karma, and in a very real and literal sense it is the most lawful of all laws governing humankind.

Karma is a Sanskrit word that means action. It is associated with cause and effect and the fact that each individual is constantly meeting the consequences of her or his previous choices. Although the workings of karma are repeatedly illustrated in scripture, generally most students of the Bible overlook or simply don't recognize the information as being applicable to the law of karma. However, phrases such as, "Thou hast been in Eden the garden of God . . . Thou wast perfect in thy ways from the day that thou wast created, till iniquity was found in thee" (Ezekiel 28:13, 15); "He that leadeth into captivity shall go into captivity . . . " (Revelation 13:10); " . . . with what measure ye mete, it shall be measured to you again," (Matthew 7:2, Mark 4:24, Luke 6:38) and, Jesus' statement that " . . . all they that take the sword shall perish with the sword" (Matthew 26:52), for example, are just a few of the many biblical examples that clearly describe the consequential activity of karmic law.[1]

Sometimes individuals who are new to the law of karma and the process in which reincarnation works may protest that these concepts appear to mitigate the divine gift of free will; actually, however, the reverse is true. Without karma and reincarnation, the inequities of life seem to become the ultimate responsibility of the Creator and free will is only ours in attempting to deal with what God has apparently randomly bestowed upon us. At the very least, this short-sighted understanding would suggest that free will is not all that free, and ultimately it would indicate that a fair and all-loving Creator is not as fair and all-loving as we would hope Him to be.

According to famed world religion scholar Huston Smith, rather than undermining freedom of choice, karma instead assures the exacting nature of free will, a completely moral universe, and total personal responsibility:

> Each individual is wholly responsible for his or her present condition and will have exactly the future he or she is now creating. Most people are not willing to admit this. They prefer, as the psychologists say, to project—to locate the source of their difficulties outside themselves. They want excuses, someone to blame that they may be exonerated . . . [However,] Everybody gets exactly what is deserved . . .   (Smith, pg. 64)

Similarly, Rudolf Steiner (1861–1925), the great Austrian philosopher, educator, and founder of the Anthroposophical Society, connected an individual's karmic experiences with absolute personal freedom of choice:

> So, in the last analysis, it is we who with the highest part of our being have willed our karma. Whenever we bemoan our destiny on earth and complain of our ill-fortune, we are railing against *our own choice,* not the choice of some arbitrary god or gods who have done us a bad turn. In consequence, the one vice from which no one with knowledge of karma should permit himself is envy, either envy of anyone else's life situation, or of his talents, fortune or friends. For we have what we have chosen and earned, and what is good for us. Here our earthly freedom begins. We can, as we say so truly, "make the best of" our circumstances; we can fully accept them in the knowledge that they are what we need for our spiritual progress. We have built our house, and now it is our task to live in it.
>
> (Easton, pg. 156)

Sometimes, even proponents of reincarnation and karma have a difficult time accepting the responsibility of actions committed by a "former self" in previous lives. However, when this occurs, it generally entails the perspective of a mere seven to ten decades in activity, rather than seeing the soul's various experiences as one continuous existence. The Hindu proverb of the mango tree clearly illustrates the nature of this continuity:

> There was a kingdom in which one man was caught stealing a mango from another man's property. The property owner obtained an audience with the king and brought the thief with him before the monarch to receive justice. Immediately, the thief proclaimed his innocence:
>
> "Your Majesty, I am not guilty of a crime for I did not take this man's mango—the one he planted in the ground is different than the one I took. I have committed no crime for his mango remains where he planted it."
>
> However, the king agreed with the property owner stating, "You are guilty because the last mango resulted from the first one. The one you took is a continuation of the one that was planted."

In spite of this illustration of individual continuity, some people might then protest, "Well then, why don't I remember my past lives?" The truth of the matter, however, is that countless individuals have been able to become consciously aware of their own past lives, and all individuals actually do remember at an unconscious level. In terms of acquiring a conscious awareness, numerous books like Carol Bowman's *Children's Past-lives*, Brian Weiss's *Only Love Is Real*, and decades of research by individuals like Dr. Ian Stephenson, author of *Twenty Cases Suggestive of Reincarnation*, all confirm that people from all walks of life and backgrounds have been able to discover the reality of reincarnation and karma in their personal lives.

In terms of an unconscious awareness, each individual's biases, talents, fears, expectations, and thoughts and opinions of other cultures, races, religions, and time periods in history, often have roots in unconscious memories of past-life experiences. In addition, because the law of karma is inextricably woven to the nature of humankind, throughout history an unconscious awareness of this law has also resulted in depictions of karma in the world's religious scriptures, in legend, in archetypal or universal stories, in fairy tales, and in myth.

Certainly one of the most famous mythic depictions of how an individual is unable to escape her or his "karmic fate" is told in the story of Oedipus. In brief, Oedipus was born to the king and queen of Thebes. The couple's joy over the birth of their baby was short-lived when it was prophesied that their son was destined to kill his father and marry his mother. In order to avert the prophecy, the couple ordered their child taken away and killed. A servant carried the infant out of the city, but rather than following orders the servant took pity and simply abandoned the baby in the forest—leaving the boy's fate to the whims of the gods and the elements.

Shortly thereafter the infant was found by a shepherd, who took the babe to Corinth. The boy was immediately adopted by the king and queen of Corinth, as they had no children of their own. The child was named Oedipus and was raised as a prince in the city, unaware of his background or adoption.

When Oedipus reached adulthood, he consulted the Oracle at Delphi about his destiny. When the Oracle proclaimed that he was fated to kill his father and marry his mother, Oedipus vowed to leave Corinth as a means of averting the prophecy. He journeyed to Thebes and en route argued with and subsequently killed a wealthy traveler. Unbeknownst to him, it was the king of Thebes—his own father. After his arrival in Thebes, a winged sphinx monster continually threatened the city. Because the people lived in such fear, the citizens declared that whoever defeated the monster would be married to the widowed queen and elevated to the stature of king. The task finally fell to Oedipus, who killed the monster and married the queen, unwittingly fulfilling the second half of the prophecy and his own fate by marrying his birth mother.

The consequential activity of karmic law is also clearly illustrated in a variety of biblical examples, including Jesus' parable of the talents:

> For the kingdom of heaven is as a man travelling into a far country, who called his own servants, and delivered unto them his goods.
>
> And unto one he gave five talents, to another two, and to another one; to every man according to his several ability; and straightway took his journey.
>
> Then he that had received the five talents went and traded with the same, and made them other five talents.
>
> And likewise he that had received two, he also gained other two.
>
> But he that had received one went and digged in the earth, and hid his lord's money.
>
> After a long time the lord of those servants cometh, and reckoneth with them.
>
> And so he that had received five talents came and brought other five talents, saying, Lord, thou deliveredst unto me five talents: behold, I have gained beside them five talents more.
>
> His lord said unto him, Well done, thou good and faithful servant: thou hast been faithful over a few things, I will make thee ruler over many things: enter thou into the joy of thy lord.
>
> He also that had received two talents came and said, Lord, thou deliveredst unto me two talents: behold, I have gained two other talents beside them.
>
> His lord said unto him, Well done, good and faithful servant; thou hast been faithful over a few things, I will make thee ruler over many things: enter thou into the joy of thy lord.
>
> Then he which had received the one talent came and said, Lord, I knew thee that thou art an hard man, reaping where thou hast not sown, and gathering where thou hast not strawed:
>
> And I was afraid, and went and hid thy talent in the earth: lo, there thou hast that is thine.
>
> His lord answered and said unto him, Thou wicked and

slothful servant, thou knewest that I reap where I sowed not, and gather where I have not strawed:

Thou oughtest therefore to have put my money to the exchangers, and then at my coming I should have received mine own with usury.

Take therefore the talent from him, and give it unto him which hath ten talents.

For unto every one that hath shall be given, and he shall have abundance: but from him that hath not shall be taken away even that which he hath.

And cast ye the unprofitable servant into outer darkness: there shall be weeping and gnashing of teeth.

(Matthew 25:14-30)

Rather than suggesting that God is threatening to send an individual to hell if she or he isn't financially responsible, or that the divine is somehow concerned with the quantity of "talents" (or money) that an individual can procure, the parable instead depicts the consequential activity of individual choice, will, and activity. In other words, life is a completely lawful experience that "rewards" or "reprimands" individual behavior. To be sure, some might simply see the parable as describing the "ultimate" reward or punishment occurring after earthly life, but if this is the case why did the servant with the two talents not receive the exact same reward as the servant with five? Along these same lines, why would a servant who simply came across as being lazy, ignorant, or fearful receive eternal damnation? Rather than suggesting that there are various levels of reward in Heaven or that lazy people might go to hell, Jesus is instead describing the exacting nature of the law in terms of cause and effect. This law is also known as the law of karma.

This same lawfulness is reflected in a variety of myths and fairy tales, as well as individuals' responses to those stories in terms of their subconscious expectation that in the end everything will turn out lawful, just, for the best, and even "happily ever after." Otherwise, the story just doesn't "feel" right. In other words, there is an innate understanding and expectation that the laws governing the universe are completely orderly and that everyone eventually gets exactly what he or she deserves. An understanding of this law is illustrated in innumerable classics that have been passed down from one generation to another. Whether it's the fact that Dorothy finally returns home in the *Wizard of Oz*, in spite of numerous obstacles; or that Cinderella, rather than one of her stepsisters, marries the prince; or that Frodo eventually overthrows the dark lord Sauron and the ring of power, we are comforted by the fact that the universe is completely lawful.

However, in spite of this innate understanding of the lawfulness of life, even individuals who are familiar with the term "karma" are often mistaken as to what it actually means. Karma is not a debt, it is not a punishment, it is not an inescapable fate, it is not really something that exists "between" people, and ultimately it is not even "good" or "bad" in character. Karma is simply an interactive, energetic force that is set in motion through our intent, desire, thought, deed, and word, and as a result molds and shapes the resulting consequence of all our actions. It is a universally applicable and dynamic constant that is interwoven with everything associated with being human.

With this in mind, twentieth-century Christian mystic Edgar Cayce (1877-1945) suggested that karma might be more closely understood as memory. Rather than being a debt between people or even an unchangeable destiny, Cayce believed that karma was more like a pool of unconscious memory that was drawn upon by an individual and influenced his or her choices. To be sure, this karmic memory could affect experiences and relationships; however, free will remained the strongest component in determining how an individual experienced his or her life.

Called "the father of holistic medicine" and "the most documented psychic of all time," Cayce became known for his incredible accuracy and for a psychic legacy that continues to help and inspire individuals the world over, long after his death. Since the publication of Cayce's first biography in 1943, *There Is a River*, literally hundreds of books have been written about his life and work. In addition to his information on health and intuition, Cayce became known for his insights into ancient history, ecumenical spirituality, dream interpretation, and for being one of the first individuals in the Western Hemisphere to thoroughly explore the workings of reincarnation, karma, and the journey of the soul.[2]

In outlining how karmic law operated in individuals' lives, Cayce once told a twenty-three-year-old Christian student studying electrical engineering that it might actually be compared to the body's assimilation process. Once assimilated, this memory could then be said to have an influence upon a person's destiny, for it was something that had to be met within the individual. Its activity also exemplified, according to Cayce, the scientific lawfulness of cause and effect:

> Well that karma be understood, and how it is to be met. For, in various thought—whether considered philosophy or religion, or whether from the more scientific manner of cause and effect—karma is all of these and more.
>
> Rather it may be likened unto a piece of food, whether fish or bread, taken into the system; it is assimilated by the organs of digestion, and then those elements that are gathered from same are made into the forces that flow through the body, giving the strength and vitality to an animate object, or being, or body.
>
> So, in experiences of a soul, in a body, in an experience in the earth. Its thoughts make for that upon which the soul feeds . . .
>
> Then, the soul re-entering into a body under a different environ either makes for the expending of that it has made through the experience in the sojourn in a form that is called in some religions as destiny of the soul, in another philosophy that which has been builded must be met in some way or manner, or in the more scientific manner that a certain cause produces a certain effect.
>
> Hence we see that karma is *all* of these and more.   440-5[3]

When a twenty-seven-year-old woman asked for further clarification as to what kind of "karmic debt" existed between herself and various family members, Cayce suggested that she had the concept all wrong. Rather than being a debt *between* people, in reality karma was a debt with self. To be sure, this debt was often worked out in association with others, but an individual's karma (or memory) was connected to her or him alone. The woman was told:

> . . . What *is* karmic debt? This ye have made a bugaboo! This ye have overbalanced within thyself! . . . it is merely self being *met*, in relationships to that they *themselves* are working out and not a karmic debt between but a karmic debt of self that may be worked out between the associations that exist in the present! And this is true for every soul.   1436-3

In addition, rather than seeing karma as some miserable burden that would forever mar an individual's life, Cayce told a forty-seven-year-old housewife that the way in which she met her karmic memory actually determined her life's experience. It was not that karma somehow set in stone her destiny, rather what was most important was how she used her free will in relationship to that karmic memory. For the woman and others, the attitude and will was the greatest determinant in each individual's unfolding life experience:

> These may become stepping-stones or stumbling blocks, according to what one may do about one's ideals in the present . . .
> But no urge, no karmic force even surpasses the will of the entity in any given experience or choice to be made!
> For Life is continuous, and is Infinite!
> Then, the retardment or advancement of each soul—as this entity—depends upon how well it comprehends or applies its understanding.   1554-2

The use of the will plays an important role in life because each individual is a complex combination of positive traits as well as negative patterns that potentially come into play in every experience and every relationship encounter. All individuals have the capacity to choose to emulate the very best they have within themselves or the very worst.

Taken to an extreme, each of these choices, made positively or negatively, one at a time, over a long period of time, could ultimately lead to someone becoming very good or very evil. In addition, in terms of personal relationships, individuals sometimes have both positive and negative past-life patterns and karmic memories in connection with the very same person.

For example, in 1943 a husband and wife each obtained their own past-life reading from Edgar Cayce. The wife was given a series of lifetimes, including two in which she had known her present-day husband. In one of those incarnations she had been in the Holy Land and had been greatly influenced by the Apostle Paul, becoming a healer and a woman of great faith. She was also given a lifetime in ancient Egypt in which she had served in one of the healing temples (3478-2). Other incarnations included being a nurse and working with spiritual healing.

Conversely, the husband, an osteopath, was given a series of his own lifetimes and was told that the two having the greatest bearing on him at the time of the reading were those in which he had known his wife—in the Holy Land and in Egypt (3360-1). During the Holy Land experience, he had also been involved in the early Christian movement at the same time as his wife but had been fearful of persecution, causing him to eventually forsake his interest. This experience apparently caused him to distrust his wife (perhaps out of a fear that she could have divulged his one-time affiliation) and her to distrust him (perhaps wondering how genuine his interest had been in the first place). That distrust remained with them at the level of karmic memory.

During the husband's lifetime in ancient Egypt, he had been a member of the king's inner circle and had been present whenever discussions arose regarding the dissemination of ideas related to the health of body, mind, and spirit. In that capacity he had apparently come into contact with his present wife, as she had been involved in a similar healing work. They got together, becoming very close in that experience. He had also experienced a lifetime as a Native American healer who drew upon the medicinal properties of herbs. To be sure, both husband and wife had a variety of karmic memories related to healing work.

Cayce informed the couple that because of their common interest in healing, they could have been very close but had learned to doubt one another in the Holy Land. In order to deal with these two seemingly opposing karmic memories—being close and at the same time having an air of distrust—they were advised to draw upon the positive memory from their Egyptian experience as a source of inspiration and helpfulness. During that period they had both been involved in the healing of body, mind, and spirit in service to others and it was something they were encouraged to continue in the present. The wife was told that she possessed an innate ability to work with prayer and spiritual healing, such as laying-on-of-hands, and her physician-husband admitted his own interest in spiritual healing. It's important to point out that it wasn't really necessary for them to consciously remember their former lifetimes in Egypt. Instead, by picking up talents, strengths, and interests that they had shared at the present time, they could apparently draw upon their positive karmic memory with one another and overcome the negative one.

Conversely, an example of the negative expression of karmic memory occurred in the life of a middle-aged woman in her fifties named Bonnie Rosen.[4] The mother of eight grown children, Bonnie had always been extremely close to her son Isaac. Although mother and son had incarnated together on a number of occasions, one of their strongest connections had occurred during the time of the Old Testament character Aaron. During that period, mother and son had been connected as wife and husband, and the close bond they had felt for one another continued into the present, at least until Isaac got married.

Because of her deep feelings of attachment, Bonnie was not at all friendly with Isaac's wife. Obviously, at an unconscious level, part of her felt replaced by the younger woman. Over time, Bonnie became so resentful of Isaac's wife that friends even noted how absurd the situation had become. An enthusiast of the Cayce material, Bonnie had a number of readings, including readings for cancer, which eventually developed. On a number of occasions, she made it very clear to Edgar Cayce that she didn't want her daughter-in-law finding out about her condition: " . . . I want no meddling in of [my daughter-in-law]. If you ever send any of my readings to his [my son's] house, you and I won't be friends," (325-51) and "I do not want my readings to go to his home, as she [my daughter-in-law] is the fault of all my illness." (325-60)

Rather than thinking that the situation was simply because of a negative past-life experience with the daughter-in-law, Isaac's wife eventually told Edgar Cayce's secretary, Gladys Davis, that she was certain that the two of them could have been friends had they met under different circumstances. After all, the two women came from similar backgrounds and social circles. Notations in Bonnie Rosen's file suggest instead that she had misdirected her memory of a closeness she had felt for her son in their previous relationship and had become jealous when someone else took the place she had formerly held. After Bonnie's death, Gladys noted in the files: "The attachment to her son was so great . . . there was no room left for his wife for her affection in this incarnation." (325-63 Report File) This case suggests that although the karmic memory of love and the close bond that mother and son had shared could have enabled the two to love one another unconditionally, instead Bonnie's attitude and choices led her to become resentful and jealous. Undoubtedly, her response led to additional karmic memory for her in relationship to both her son and her daughter-in-law—memory that will have to be met at some point in the future.

A fascinating example of meeting karmic memory in a family relationship occurred in the life experience of Carol and William Sloan—a married couple that had been together for eighteen years. It was Carol who requested the reading, asking Edgar Cayce for help in dealing with her situation that she described as follows:

Dear Mr. Cayce:
I have had a number of people speak to me of your remarkable and precise work . . . There has been a long history of emotional tension which I have more or less taken care of thru meditation. One aspect of the tension is due to 18 years of married life with no physical connection with my husband. He has always been impotent thru no fault of his. There is simply not the physical development necessary. I do not think

it necessary to go into the reasons why I stayed with him all these years. There was a few laisons [liaisons] on my part at first until I found the Arcane School & received its very fine instructions in meditation.

I got along very well, considering, until a former suitor came precipitately into my life last Fall. He is now married (nearly 10 years). From the minute we met again, the flame came back to him in its full intensity, AND I responded. I am trying to release us—but I find my health going down . . . I SEEK TO KEEP VERY BUSY. One doctor said since the periphery veins on my legs showed a tendency to "breaking," I needed the female hormone Estrogen . . . I fear to take it in case it would increase my feminine desire . . .

My husband knows I am asking you for help—but HE DOES NOT know the situation . . . I would not leave my husband for a number of reasons which you may see, and also, he has evolved into a very beautiful character . . .

2329-1 Background Information

One of the woman's questions included the following: "Would a liaison with some trusted friend help me so I could function positively and rhythmically in carrying on the normal business of home life and work?" She added, "I hesitate because he has a wife and I LIKE her . . . I don't want to hurt anyone."

During the course of the woman's reading, Edgar Cayce described the events and the karmic memory that had led to the present situation. Apparently, in a previous life during the Crusades the couple had also been together. At the time, the husband felt a calling to go off and fight in the Holy War. One of his worries, however, concerned his wife's fidelity and the fact that he could not trust her to remain faithful until his return. As a result he forced her into wearing a chastity belt. Obviously, the situation had lawfully resulted in his being impotent in the present. In other words, since he had once attempted to control someone else sexually, the karmic memory of that situation had drawn to him the experience of being controlled (or perhaps losing control) at the level of his own sexuality.

Had the situation stopped there, the karmic memory might have been his alone, but the readings suggest instead that the woman began to hate her husband with a vengeance, swearing to eventually seek her revenge. The act of hate, anger and uncontrolled frustration created a karmic memory of its own:

> This brought periods of disturbing forces of many natures; the determining to sometime, somewhere, be free, and to "get even . . . "
>
> . . . the forcing to remain in a state of chastity brought detrimental determinations to the entity.
>
> That these have and do become portions of the entity's experience, then, is only the meeting of self.   2329-1

In other words, the woman had drawn to herself a situation that would enable her meet a similar period of "chastity" and yet overcome the hatred and vengeful attitude she had once held toward her husband. Rather than seeing the experience as a miserable burden, Cayce advised the wife that she had the ability to view her situation as an "opportunity" to meet herself. He added: "Know that the birthright of every soul is choice, or will." With that in mind, he also provided her with suggestions for working on her relationship with her husband and for interacting with her former boyfriend in a way that would not adversely affect either of them in terms of their spiritual ideals. After receiving the information, the woman wrote back:

> Thank you so much for the VERY helpful Life Reading. I've read it over and over and much is made clear to me. As you say, at first reading one can not get all the implications, but gradually it reveals itself. Your reading gave me REAL help in regard to the tie between my husband and myself.

As is evidenced in each of these cases, from the standpoint of the Edgar Cayce material karmic memory is essentially an unconscious reservoir of information. Although this memory may draw certain events and individuals to one another, the way in which an individual responds to that memory determines her or his actual life experience. Through the process of exploring stories such as these and the life choices and experiences of others we may gain insights into the ways in which free will and individual attitude can literally create personal destiny. By observing the successful experience of others in meeting their personal karma through choice and application, it's possible to become inspired about meeting our own. Conversely, by witnessing the mistakes of others we might avoid similar problems in our own lives.

This book was written in an attempt to examine the workings of karma, especially as it plays out in the dynamics of family relationships. Rather than drawing attention to the consequential activity of personal karma, it is hoped that it might instead illustrate the lawfulness of life, the exacting nature of individual responsibility, and the ever-present hopefulness of personal free will. In the end, perhaps it might make some small contribution to humanity's understanding of the fact that life is a completely lawful experience and that God is truly as fair and as loving as we have always wished for our Creator to be.

1

Edgar Cayce on Family Karma

For indeed the laws are ever, "As ye sow, so shall ye reap—as ye mete it to thy fellow man, so will it be meted to thee again." Individuals constantly meet themselves, then.

And when they, as the story of old, blame someone else it is the continuous warring within themselves. For their selves, their consciousness, their soul, knows! 1538-1

"I always had a very difficult time in my relationship with my father," reported Karen Turner when she was in her sixties, "at least until I was an adult with a family of my own. Growing up, I was very much afraid of him, and he always made it very clear to me that I was not his favorite daughter." Conversely, Karen absolutely worshipped her mother: "I just loved her. She was such a wise teacher. If you had a question, she would talk to you in a way that the answer eventually came out of your own mouth. She was really good with children and young people."

Karen and her younger sister, Arlene, were raised by their parents, Jim and Barbara, in Princess Anne County, Virginia. The girls loved dancing, both performance dancing and dancing in groups. When the two were growing up there were lots of opportunities to go to dances with groups of other kids. Karen recalls that the dances were just one activity that illustrated the different kind of relationship each girl shared with her father:

> Whenever I asked my dad if the two of us could go dancing,
> without even thinking about it he would respond with an
> absolute, "No!" However, if Arlene asked him if we could go
> dancing he would say yes immediately. Even as a child this
> became so obvious to me that whenever Arlene and I wanted
> to do anything, we got my sister to ask for the two of us.

Jim also came across as very domineering and controlling with his
wife. The couple had a difficult relationship and there was a time when
Barbara even had a nervous breakdown. In modern terminology they
might have been called co-dependent, as they seemed to be unable to
get along and yet also unable to do without the other.

Complicating the family situation was the fact that Jim and Barbara
had become very close to another couple, Bradley and Vicki. Perhaps it
was due to the challenges in her own marriage that Barbara found herself completely drawn to Bradley and he found himself drawn to her.
Looking back, Karen can even remember an occasion as a child when
she and her mother accompanied Bradley to the beach: "He had his
daughter with him and I remember how my mother and he just talked
and talked, and kept looking at one another. Even then, it seemed quite
unusual to me." In time, rumors circulated that Barbara and Bradley
were having an affair, causing Jim and Vicki to sever all ties between the
two couples.

Through a friend, Barbara heard about the work of Edgar Cayce.
Thinking that a reading might at least help to make her home life more
"congenial," she sought Cayce's help in the spring of 1940. The information proved to be so insightful that within a matter of months Barbara
had obtained readings for her husband and her two daughters. Even
Jim became interested in the material. The story presents a truly fascinating example of the dynamics of family karma.

According to the family's information, each of them had been together during the 1600s in Williamsburg, Virginia. It was in that time
and place that much of the family's karmic memory had been created.

The readings stated that Jim had been instrumental in the Williamsburg community as essentially a farmer and an individual who was skilled with the distribution of supplies and materials for the other settlers. During that experience, his name had been Monroe Grossman.

Monroe was a respected member of his community and the father of one disobedient daughter named Sarah. Seen as being somewhat rebellious and wild even as a child by the conservative Williamsburg community, Sarah had been nicknamed "the little Indian." According to the readings, when Sarah reached young womanhood she created "some disturbing conditions" through her actions (2175-3). Apparently, she created quite a scandal by her free nature and, to his horror, Monroe eventually discovered that his unwed daughter was pregnant. It made for an interesting example of karmic cause-and-effect to learn that Sarah had returned as Barbara and that Bradley had been the same young man from the Williamsburg lifetime with whom she had had the affair.

Because of his daughter's actions, Monroe essentially abandoned Sarah, evicting her from his home. It was clear that he wanted her to face the dire consequences of her actions. To his great disgust and anger, another Williamsburg woman took pity on Sarah and invited the young girl to live with her. The cause of Jim's antagonism toward his daughter Karen became clear when it was learned that Karen had once been the woman who had volunteered to help the pregnant Sarah.

Arlene's role in the karmic situation was that she had also been a member of the Williamsburg community and very close to Monroe Grossman, who was apparently a widower. It appeared that Arlene had been her father's girlfriend in their most recent lifetime together, certainly explaining why she had always been Jim's favorite.

To be sure, the family's karmic connection was not limited to the 1600s or Williamsburg. Karen and Arlene had both been involved in music and the arts during an Egyptian lifetime. Actually, the two girls had frequently been involved in entertaining, music, and dance throughout a number of their respective incarnations, explaining their intense attraction to entertaining and dance in the present. Interestingly enough, both girls would grow to become even more involved in performance dance—the two often working together. In time, because of her aptitude Arlene even won a scholarship to study dance at Carnegie Hall.

Jim learned that he had been connected to Barbara in a number of previous lifetimes, most notably Williamsburg, Palestine and Atlantis. In Palestine, the two had been married and very close, contributing to their desire to be reacquainted in the Williamsburg experience where things had not turned out quite so well. In Atlantis the two had also apparently been close but their differing opinions and extended circle of friends had been quite different, and those differences had contributed to the father–daughter problems in seventeenth–century Williamsburg. Jim was also told that he had known each of his daughters in a variety of other experiences, and each of those experiences contributed both positively and negatively to his overall relationship with them in the present.

During a follow–up reading, Jim inquired how the long ago past influenced an individual in the present. The answer came that past lives contributed to an individual's faults and virtues and were drawn upon in the present when an individual was able to deal with the memory of those influences. Cayce used the analogy of going to school to explain how that memory actually worked in an individual's life:

> This may be comparable to the experience of an entity as it undertakes its studies, its lessons, in school. Not that there is in the everyday life the remembering of daily experiences in school, yet those daily experiences create the background with which the entity—as in its daily contact with problems—reviews in a memory those problems that were part of the experience during such days of what is commonly called education, or unfoldment.
>
> Just so in the daily experience of an individual entity through the various lessons learned, gained or lost in the earthly experiences, it builds a background to which the entity-mind responds as it applies itself in meeting the daily problems that arise.
>
> One may ask, as this entity—*why*, then, does one not

recall more often those experiences?

The same may be asked of why there is not the remember-
ing of the time when two and two to the entity became four, or
when C A T spelled cat. It always did! Ye only became aware
of same as it became necessary for its practical application in
the experience!   2301-4

During her own follow-up reading, Barbara asked for further insights
into some of the problems she was still experiencing in the present. She
was told that both Bradley and Vicki had been her close friends during
the Williamsburg experience. Bradley had been the one with whom she
had had the affair, and Vicki had been a young woman much like herself who often engaged in what Cayce called "questionable experiences"
for the time. Although Barbara and Jim were no longer in contact with
the other couple, when she asked what her attitude toward Bradley
should be in the present, the response came: "loving indifference." Apparently, it would be the easiest way for her to work out her karmic
situation with Jim. When she asked how she could help the couples
reconcile their friendship, she was encouraged to let it happen naturally as an outgrowth of living in the same vicinity rather than attempting to fix the problem; otherwise her motives would be questioned.

Barbara also asked how her daughter Karen had helped her during
the Williamsburg experience. Cayce replied that after her questionable
relationships as Sarah, and becoming pregnant, Karen essentially enabled her mother to begin her life anew, "by bringing the entity into her
own home, into her *own* activities, into her *own* relationships, see?" (2175–
3) Barbara also inquired as to why she felt so strongly that unwed mothers needed help and sympathy. The response was obvious: "You were
almost one yourself, if you hadn't been picked up!" Apparently in the
Williamsburg experience, Sarah Grossman had found a husband before
ever giving birth to her child.

In time, the readings for all of the family members proved especially
helpful in explaining how the karmic situation had been created, as
well as providing guidance as to how it could be overcome in the
present. Years later, Barbara would tell author Gina Cerminara, who was

compiling an article about the efficacy of the Cayce work,[5] that the readings had made sense out of the entire experience for her. She understood that Jim had become domineering in an effort to prevent her
from becoming "wayward" in the present. Although their marriage had
begun with a pattern of dominance and resentment, in time their situation was met in love and understanding and the couple was able to
overcome those personality traits that had once caused friction. The
readings had counseled Barbara and Jim to take time to focus on their
personal and home life. They were encouraged to work on self-devel-
opment, becoming more involved in things of a spiritual nature. It was
also recommended that they find balance in their life together: "Take
time for play, take time for recreation, take time for physical, mental
and spiritual development." (2301-2) Eventually when habitual patterns
(such as Jim's dominance) began to arise, they were met with "detachment and a sense of humor." The article ended with the notation that,
"the marriage has become harmonious, with both partners seeking to
cooperate in building soul qualities . . . " (2175-3 Report File)

The last two family members to work through the family karma were
Karen and her father. Karen admits that it wasn't really until after she
had a family of her own and her mother had died of breast cancer that
she and her father were truly able to work on their relationship together. As time passed, the two became ever closer. Karen says that she
was eventually able to understand her father and why he had become
the kind of person she had experienced as a child. His demeanor was
due not only to his past-life experiences but also to his upbringing and
being essentially abandoned through the death of both of his parents
when he was only a child. It proved to be just one more interesting
karmic payback since he had once abandoned his own daughter during
his life as Monroe Grossman. According to Karen, long before her
father's death they had managed to work through their Williamsburg
karma, overcoming any remaining misunderstanding or antagonism,
so that Karen could say without hesitation, "We were very close and I
truly loved him."

Years later when Karen was asked how she felt she, her sister, and her
parents had all worked through their various karmic connections and

entanglements, she replied simply, "very well." In the end, all family members had learned from one another and become better people for having had the opportunity of being together.

As suggested by the story of Karen Turner, her sister, and her parents, family relationships are essentially an archaeological dig of past-life experiences, patterns, and relationships that influence present-day interactions within each family. Like a reservoir of unconscious memory these influences definitely have an affect in terms of predisposing each family member to various feelings, inclinations and experiences, but free will remains the strongest determinant of the outcome that memory has on the individual in the present. On one occasion a couple seeking a joint life reading and marital advice from Edgar Cayce was told that, regardless of whether or not a past-life connection had been a positive experience, karmic memory often attracted individuals together. However, what two people did with that memory and their relationship in the present was most dependent upon the will and the application of spiritual ideals:

> All entities—as these two entities—meet for a purpose . . .
> Whether these have been for weal or woe does not prevent the
> attraction. Thus, whether that attraction is to be for the ad-
> vancement or the undoing of something in themselves de-
> pends, again, upon what is the ideal of each.   2533-7

From the perspective of the Cayce information, life's relationships and experiences are drawn to an individual in an effort to assist that soul in becoming a better person, eventually becoming aligned to a pattern of spiritual perfection. When a thirty-eight-year-old man once asked Cayce about the rationale behind the law of rebirth, the response came: "The Creator intended man to be a companion with Him . . . How many [lifetimes] will it require for thee to be able to be a companion with the Creative Forces where ever you are?" (416-18) In other words, the purpose of life is not simply to be born into a family, go to school, get a job, acquire material goods, create a family of one's own, grow older and then eventually die, leaving one's descendents and family members to repeat the very same cycle. Instead, the purpose of life is to go through a series of experiences that will eventually enable the soul to awaken to its ultimate level of spiritual awareness. On one occasion, that level of awareness was described as "the awareness within each soul, imprinted in pattern on the mind and waiting to be awakened by the will, of the soul's oneness with God." (5749-14) Awakening to that level of conscious awareness is the destiny of each and every soul.

In Cayce's cosmology it is through an ongoing process of personal spiritual growth and development that each individual learns, grows and constantly meets self—self's past experiences, relationships, inclinations, talents, and faults in the form of karmic memory. With this in mind, when a twenty-two-year-old man once asked Edgar Cayce, "From which side of my family do I inherit most?" The reply came: "You have inherited most from yourself, not from family! The family is only a river through which it (the entity, soul) flows!" (1233-1)

Rather than believing that karma created an unavoidable or inevitable destiny, Edgar Cayce instead saw karmic memory as simply an influence or an impulse. In fact, on one occasion when discussing karma in a reading given to a thirty-five-year-old bookkeeper Cayce stated, "What is karma but giving way to impulse?" (622-6) suggesting that free will always remained the strongest determinant in creating an individual's actual life experience as individuals always had the choice not to fall into old habit patterns. The importance of the human will in co-creating one's life is clearly illustrated in the karmic situation of the Merrill family—a family of three individuals, each of whom obtained life readings from Edgar Cayce in 1938. By some accounts, the family was not very close. Apparently the Merrill family was prone to arguments, willfulness and even personal excess, especially in terms of alcohol. Their story, excerpted from the Cayce archives is essentially as follows:

The father's name was Stephen; he was a forty-four-year-old advertising executive. The mother was Eliza—a forty-year-old housewife. The couple had one child—an eleven-year-old boy named Samuel. In addition to discovering their past lives, they hoped to understand their present talents and abilities as well as hear about any weaknesses that needed to be worked on. Because Cayce's perspective of karma is exacting and individualized—in other words two people may come together to resolve karmic memory but each might be working on something entirely different—an overview of the Merrill's various karmic connections is told primarily from the point-of-view of the couple's son.

During the course of the reading, Edgar Cayce described Samuel's innate strengths and weaknesses, as well as some of the previous life experiences in which those traits had also been evident. Perhaps surprisingly, the reading began by warning the parents that their child would be prone to drink and that alcohol would be a tremendous temptation. In fact, each of their life readings suggested that all three had experienced lifetimes in ancient Egypt thousands of years previously when some of the temples had turned away from the practice of the healing arts and instead began taking part in excesses of every immoral nature. Perhaps it was this same experience that resulted in a warning to Samuel's parents that their son would be prone to loose morality. In spite of the warning, however, the readings assured the couple that proper guidance directed toward the raising of their son would enable this tendency to be worked through and overcome, enabling the boy to become grounded and live out a productive life.

When the parents asked how they were doing in terms of raising their son in a constructive manner, Eliza was told that, at the time of the reading, she was being very helpful (1602-4). Similarly, Stephen Merrill was informed that he had an innate ability to work with young people as a helpful and inspiring influence and had, as a matter of fact, served in a similar capacity during an incarnation at the time of Alexander the Great (1564-1). What was important for both parents to keep in mind was that rather than preaching at their son, they needed to guide and direct him by their own example.

The couple was told that the most recent past life having a bearing on their son's present was as a fundamentalist minister in Massachusetts, during the same period in which Stephen had been a frontiersman and trapper. During that experience, Samuel had been raised by rather stern and severe parents, which resulted in him becoming somewhat severe and stern in his own outlook. Although he had gained in spiritual growth during the experience because of his service to others, the same experience had made him prone to be judgmental of others. That lifetime had also given him a love of routine as well as further cultivated his soul talents in the areas of writing and music. The boy's lifetime as a minister had reinforced the soul's tendency to be somewhat argumentative and willful, to which the parents were advised: "Hence the necessity of using love, patience, forbearance and longsuffering in the *directing* of that as would be the change of the mind of the entity through especially the next two or three, yes four years." (1581–1)

Prior to his life as a minister, Samuel had been a member of the Jewish priesthood during the rule of the Roman Empire. In that experience, one of his chief duties had been to blow the ram's horn, announcing various services in the temple. In addition to reinforcing his love of music and his desire for structure and being connected to a religious order, the experience had been rich with ritual. He had also learned to be somewhat of a diplomat in that experience, but at the same time he had acquired a great love of secrecy and the habit of using information to coerce others into doing what he wanted them to do. This also created a tendency in which he was prone to be attracted to power for personal and material benefit.

In another reading given later to the boy's mother, Cayce stated that on a number of occasions Eliza, Samuel, and Stephen had each been in the earth during the same periods in history. Although they had often been connected or knew each other, sometimes they had simply been present in the same historical epoch. In other words some of the family karma each was working through in the present had been created individually, not necessarily with one another, but they had been drawn back together as a means of addressing the karmic memory that they shared in common (1602–2).

As one example, according to the readings Samuel's mother, Eliza, also had a soul tendency of being attracted to power. During the lifetime that Samuel had been engaged with the ritual of the Jewish temple service, Eliza had been a member of the Jewish community but employed by the Romans as one who gathered information for the purpose of tax assessment. She had been drawn to the Roman authority because of their power. This tendency had also been evident previously during a Chaldean incarnation when she had been taken prisoner and eventually rose to become the wife of her captor, adopting a "queenly nature" in the process. Eliza's inclination to be attracted to those in power was described by Cayce, as follows:

> Hence we find the entity in the present is interested in and drawn towards those in high places, in many ways and manners. Not that the entity may be said to be a social climber, but one by whose natural *instincts*—as would be called in psychological language—is attracted, drawn to those who *are* in such positions . . . 1602-1

In a follow-up reading when Eliza asked whether the "visions and impressions" she had from time to time of Rome were from that experience or from another Roman incarnation, Cayce replied that they were connected to her Jewish incarnation when she had worked for the Romans: "As we find, it is rather the visioning of the experiences the entity had with those who were in authority." (1602-4) Certainly, Eliza's visions were simply a manifestation of her soul memory.

In one of Samuel's earlier incarnations on the continent of Asia, he had served as a kind of emissary of music and had become adept at using music to represent all manner of human emotion. The same period had also enabled him to become quite skilled in writing and teaching others. In fact, the boy's talents with music and writing had become a part of each of his subsequent incarnations. Interestingly enough, perhaps as a means of enabling them to learn from and be inspired by one another, the readings stated that Eliza also had a writing talent that had long been a part of her soul history and could be made manifest in the present.

Previously, each of the family members had lived incarnations in ancient Egypt. Stephen had been employed essentially as an emissary to the king, taking messages and edicts to other lands. Eliza had evidently been drawn to activities and temple services that put her in close proximity to the king and other members of the royal household. Samuel had worked in one of the temples, assisting individuals in the purification of both body and mind. Although mostly a positive experience, in was also during that period when strong drink had been brewed and the temple services had been turned for a time from the purification of individuals into debauchery and the satisfying of every carnal desire. Although not specified, their Egyptian lifetimes may have been at the root of the tendency for the entire family to be prone to personal excess.

Eliza and Stephen were also informed that they had been together during the English Crusades—an experience that had created a great deal of anxiety with Eliza when her loved ones went off to war. Interestingly enough, a fear of war had also been a part of Eliza's previous experience during the Chaldean lifetime when her husband was often drawn into war. In fact, when Eliza asked Cayce why she was so frightened of lightning, his reply was that the sound of the lightning reminded her of the sounds of war.

The entire Merrill family was encouraged to direct some of their energies into the pursuit of things of a spiritual nature and to direct "body, mind and purpose" toward the will of the Creator. Along these lines, when Eliza inquired whether or not she could attain the spiritual "illumination I am seeking," the response came: "Live it—be it, and ye will receive—as ye seek!" (1602-1)

In ending Samuel's reading and providing direction, Cayce suggested that trained aright the boy could become a genius or a protégé. The parents were encouraged to keep in mind the boy's negative tendencies and to train him by example. They were also reminded that it was through music or writing that Samuel could best make his life experience a productive one in the present:

> In those fields as a writer, or a musician, or a combination of these, may there be offered the greater opportunities for development in the present sojourn. In the music—not stringed instruments, but rather the horn or those natures of same, or the reed.

In these channels may the entity become not only mentally and morally but *spiritually* a guiding light!

But beware of those things that so easily beset . . .

For in this direction and in these channels, as we find, may the entity now known as [1581] become one of power, one of fame—yea, one of fortune.   1581-1

Shortly after receiving the reading, Stephen and Eliza thanked Edgar Cayce for his advice and stated that as far as they could tell the information had perfectly described everything they knew about their son:

Even at this early date it is possible for us to know your interpretations of his character, weaknesses and strengths, are absolutely correct. We see the tendencies you mention as already active and we feel, with the assistance you have given, we can do much to bring out the finest, overcoming the undesirable, making him thereby, a member of society worthy to work for the fulfillment of the Divine Plan for Man on Earth. Our sincere thanks to you . . . Again, thanks for your valuable and helpful services . . . "   1581-1 Report File

The following year, the youth had an additional reading and inquired about some of the visions or "flashes of past-lives" he had been seeing: "a Norseman, a Spaniard about the time of Ponce de Leon—one of being on Columbus' ship—a Roman soldier—an American Indian." (1581-2) Cayce responded by confirming the fact that many of the images were valid past-life memories: he had known and worked with the Indians during his incarnation as the Massachusetts minister—the same lifetime when he had journeyed from England to North America. He had also been a Norseman, as well as a Spaniard at the time of Ponce de Leon— incarnations that were valid but not necessarily important enough for Cayce to mention as having a meaningful bearing upon the present.

According to notations on file, for a time Samuel did focus on music by taking up the flute; he was also doing relatively well in school. One of his mother's letters to the Cayce family included the following: "[1581]

loves his new music teacher and seems to be a most satisfactory pupil, which pleases me. He is going thru some interesting little problems at school and in his mind—and I feel, handling them quite well, but I am certainly on the jump, keeping up with situations as they arise . . . "

Unfortunately, however, the proper upbringing and "teaching by example" appeared to be short-lived. One premise contained in the Edgar Cayce material is the fact that, since it is just as easy to reawaken a negative karmic pattern from the past as a positive one, individuals need to establish and work with a spiritual ideal. Actually, Cayce called the setting of spiritual ideals, the "most important experience" of every soul (357-13). Rather than focusing on emulating the positive, the Merrill's soon seemed to fall into some of their negative patterns. The souls' tendencies toward the extremes and alcohol became an ever-increasing problem. One family acquaintance eventually reported the couple drank quite heavily and that she had once heard Eliza boast "that it was nothing for them to drink a pint of whiskey before dinner, as a regular routine." (1564-3 Report File)

Perhaps due in part to the influence of alcohol, by 1949 Stephen's health had deteriorated to such an extent that he contracted tuberculosis and died. According to file notations, the illness had essentially alienated the family from others and forced them to keep pretty much to themselves. Eliza died four year later of cancer. And Samuel died of a heart attack in 1967 at the age of forty-one. The finally notation on file is from Eliza's brother in February 1969, who made the following report after Stephen, Eliza, and Samuel Merrill were all deceased:

> Don't know whether or not you are aware that the entire Merrill family has passed on. Stephen went first, about 1948 [1949], a victim of tuberculosis. Eliza followed him about four years later as a result of cancer. She had a troubled and very painful end. Finally, Samuel succumbed about two years ago (age 41) to a coronary. The Merrill's were not a very close-knit, harmonious, or homogeneous group. Family life was subject to quite a bit of strife. On the basis of unfinished business, I presume these family members will meet again. And

since my early life was so inextricably intertwined with theirs,
I suppose I will also most probably share in their future lives
and experiences.   1602-1 Report File

As is evident by the Merrill family story, each individual is composed
of a complex combination of past-life talents, faults, experiences and
relationships. Rather than suggesting that the outcome of the family's
twentieth-century life experience was destined because of their family
karma, instead the Cayce information provided a much more positive
possible outcome had free will simply been turned into more appropriate channels. Had the appropriate choices been made, Samuel might
have excelled at music and reawakened his love for structure and even
the ministry. In other words, although karmic memory may have pre-
disposed Samuel, Stephen and Eliza to certain impulses and inclinations, that karma did not determine the outcome. It was the apparent
misuse of the will that caused the family to fall into some of their negative habit patterns from the past. The Merrills, not karma, determined
the direction of their lives one choice and one decision at a time.

It is important to point out that karmic memory itself is not ultimately "good" or "bad" in character, it's simply memory. However, that
memory possesses positive and helpful components as readily as it con-
tains negative and destructive ones. That said, much of the information
in the Cayce files on family karma seems to be slanted toward the overcoming of negative karma, but this is simply due to the fact that individuals did not generally come to Edgar Cayce for help with a positive
relationship. The case history of Carol Davis illustrates an individual
with a positive karmic memory of her mother and brother, and a more
challenging memory of her father:

Carol Davis was a thirteen-year-old girl who received a reading at
the request of her father. Described as high-strung, prone to daydream,
and somewhat rebellious, Cayce began the reading by suggesting that
the information was being provided as a means of being helpful to
Carol as well as her parents as they guided, raised and educated their
child. He went on to suggest that the girl was extremely imaginative,
intuitive and even visionary; unfortunately this trait was being too of-

ten "subjugated" by the parents who apparently were trying to curb their daughter's imagination and direct her mind into more serious pursuits. Cayce's advice to the couple was to "allow a great deal more of the visions to be expressed by the entity . . . give them the opportunity for expression, and not 'preach at' the entity!" (2443-1)

When the father asked whether or not his daughter had known other family members previously and whether those associations had been "amicable and pleasant," the reading responded: "Most of those in the family have been in one or the other period of the entity's previous sojourns, or some in most every one of them. For, again, remember, as indicated—as ye sow, ye reap; and ye meet individuals in those activities."

Carol's relationship with her mother was extremely positive and was essentially a continuation of the same relationship she had once shared with the woman in Macedonia, where her present mother had also been her mother. Conversely, it was that same Macedonian experience from which frequent challenges with her father arose in the present. Apparently, her father had been some type of city authority or governor and Carol had often sided against him to the point where the two had become enemies. Cayce suggested that their frequent "tiffs" in the present were simply the continuation of the same kind of disagreements they had experienced earlier when each was "being pitted against the other." From that same past-life experience Carol had often seen her will and her decisions suppressed, oppressed and even ignored because of the fact that she was a woman. It was for that reason, the reading suggested, that Carol would attempt to use her femininity as a means of getting what she wanted instead of allowing the fact that she was a woman to be the obstacle it had once been: "For, the inclination will be to lead the opposite sex 'on' . . . "

In other incarnations in Atlantis and Persia, Carol had been closely associated with her present-day brother. Obviously, she continued that positive relationship into the present. It was also from the Atlantis lifetime that Carol's innate emotion of being "high-strung" had first developed. At that time, many people were making preparations to leave the continent because of anticipated destruction and disaster. However, rather than leaving, Carol instead chose to ignore the warnings and ended up remaining behind. Cayce added, "Hence we find latent within the present experience a dread of something, the entity knows not what; a fear of being in that position of not taking the warnings given, and yet rebelling—deep within—self against that of rule . . . "

As was often the case, the reading advised the parents to teach and nurture their daughter by example rather than by "preaching at" her, which was part of the karmic memory she shared with her father: "For, much more may be gained by love and counsel, and pleasantness, than by rebuke . . . " They were also encouraged to let her express her imagination, to pursue music, especially singing as a mode of expression, and to allow her to take part in sports, "especially tennis and such as handball, swimming, skating and the like." By so doing, Carol would be guided in the proper direction and any negative karmic memory she possessed with her father could be overcome.

Keeping in mind that relationships with individuals change throughout a soul's various incarnations in the earth, very often people have "family karma" from the past with individuals who are not necessarily part of their immediate family in the present. For example, the case history of Robert Carlson demonstrates how individuals from various karmic connections (family and otherwise) are constantly drawn to the evolving soul in the present as a means of dealing with that which had been "sown and reaped" previously.

Robert Carlson was a naval officer stationed in Norfolk, Virginia, when he had his first life reading from Edgar Cayce. Although only twenty-eight at the time, he had already been married and divorced. By his own admission, he frequently found himself drawn to all kinds of women and during the course of two readings he asked about the advisability of marriage to a number of them, their names being Willetta, Lucille, Betty, two Barbaras, Briannon, and a Kathleen. For a time, he and Kathleen were seriously dating and had even discussed the possibility of marriage—a possibility to which Kathleen's mother and stepfather were strongly opposed. After all, Robert was ten years older than their daughter; he had already been married and divorced, and he seemed to be involved with far too many women.

In his life reading, Robert was told that one of his frailties was his tendency to consort with too many women for the wrong purpose. It was a tendency that had been a part of his soul's nature for thousands of years—a karmic memory that had begun in Atlantis when he had forsaken his own spiritual beliefs in order to satisfy his carnal whims. In the language of the readings: "And these brought inharmony. These brought those periods of mental, physical—yea, spiritual disturbances that continue to be met in itself . . . even unto now." (1776-1)

His attraction to the women he asked about were traced to relationships he had had with each of them in the past, sometimes as relatives, including spouses, siblings, etc., and sometimes as associates and friends. Cayce told him: "These have crossed thy past oft." Some of the strongest past-life associations with the women he inquired about were as follows:

Willetta had been a close personal friend during Robert's most recent incarnation at the time of the colonization of America. During that lifetime, Robert had been misjudged and essentially outcast for his friendship with the Native American Indians. From that experience, Robert had learned to become somewhat judgmental of others, as well as of himself, and Willetta's acceptance of him from that period was the basic cause of his attraction to her.

The reading suggested that Lucille and he had frequently been together in essentially adversarial roles. The unresolved contention between the two in numerous experiences was the basis for the memory that drew them back together as a means of providing them with the opportunity to overcome the problems that still existed between them.

With Betty, he was told he had experienced a variety of relationships. They were drawn together in the present because they had often been in the earth at the same periods in history in places like Colonial America, Rome, Palestine, Persia, Egypt, and Atlantis. That shared soul history caused them to have much in common; however, as the reading stated, their personal, spiritual ideals were "far, far afield," from one another.

His attraction to Barbara number one was called "quite questionable," (1776-2) suggesting that the connection was mostly that of a sexual nature. Whereas Barbara number two had been with him during the Colonial America experience, apparently as a close acquaintance. In regards to Briannon, Robert was told to consider her simply "a passing fancy." In terms of his karmic connection to Kathleen, Cayce gave three periods that were having a direct bearing on the present: Palestine, Persia and Egypt. It was the Persian and Egyptian experiences, however, that were the strongest.

Four months after Robert had asked about her in his reading, Kathleen obtained a reading of her own. She specifically wanted further information on her relationship with Robert and how they could best work out their "individual problems in the present." (1981-2) She specifically wanted to know whether or not marriage might be the best way to work though their problems, in spite of the objections of her parents.

Cayce told her that the biggest obstacle the two had to overcome was the "weakness of being able to be overpowered by the personality of the other." That weakness had manifested itself in Persia when, as brother and sister, Robert had apparently convinced her to use her female charms in an effort to entrap a foreign leader. Conversely, in ancient Egypt, Kathleen had been Robert's consort and had essentially pushed him into activities of a more spiritual nature. Although helpful in terms of their joint spiritual growth, it had still involved the use of coercion and control to achieve what she wanted.

With these two experiences in mind, Cayce told Kathleen that "they each desire their own way." In terms of the couple's future, the reading assured her that it was a matter of free will. Although their karmic memory (as companions, brother-sister, and other relationships) had drawn them together, what they did with that memory was up to Kathleen and Robert alone. Depending upon their choices, as well as whether or not they worked with spiritual ideals and purposes in their relationship, a marriage between the two could either become "a beautiful companionship" or it could also be "made to the belittling of one or the other."

As if to confirm her chances of getting married to someone, Kathleen asked if there was someone else who could make her happier than

Robert. Cayce replied that there were many individuals that she could end up marrying: " . . . we might find twenty-five or thirty such, if you chose to make it so! It is what you make it!" In terms of the memory with Robert, he advised: "There is an experience to be worked out, if you want to do it now. If you have to do it sooner or later, you just as well do it now—if you want to."

Although the couple apparently stayed together for a short while, in the end they did not marry. In time, they went their separate ways. According to notes on file, in spite of the fact that Robert had been told in his readings not to marry until he got out of the service, he did marry while still enlisted. In fact, he married a woman he hadn't even known or asked about at the time of his readings. That marriage lasted seven years. He eventually divorced and married a third time.

Kathleen waited until she was twenty-nine to get married. Her report file states that she ended up marrying an engineer, moved to Pennsylvania, had three children, and was very happy. In a follow-up report sent to the Edgar Cayce Foundation in the 1970s, Kathleen reported that she felt she had lived "a very good life."

As stated previously, it's not that individuals come together as a means of forcing one another to deal with the karma that exists *between* them, instead that memory essentially resides within each individual alone. It is the relationship interaction that often causes each person to eventually face the karmic memory he or she possesses. A fascinating account of how karmic memory essentially affects the self is told in the story of Sara Peabody.

Sara Peabody was forty-six years old at the time of her Cayce reading. All her life she had been emotionally crippled with an uncontrollable fear of childbirth. By her own admission she had spent years and a fortune going to various doctors in an attempt to become healed of the condition. At her wit's end, she felt discouraged and continued to suffer great mental anguish, compounded by the fact that none of her friends understood such an irrational fear. Having no where else to turn, she eventually sent a request for help to Edgar Cayce. Her letter stated, in part:

I am almost on the eve of insanity and suicide. The most miserable woman on earth and almost a dope fiend. All my life my mother, who had suffered . . . [horribly] with birth of 6 six children, talked so much to me about pregnancy that when I married 18 years ago I was so scared of pregnancy that now I am living away from a dear sweet husband because I cannot bear to have him in my sight or near me. I have prayed and tried Psychology, Christian [Science] and Unity all to no avail. Do you think there is any hope for me. I wanted children and LOVED my husband but was so scared of sexual intercourse and now am worse than ever and as I say ready for suicide which I had planned this week when your booklet came and I am now begging in a hopeless, pitiful way for help—I am so melancholy all the time that suicide will have to come unless a ray of hope appears soon. If in any way you can help me PLEASE, PLEASE ANSWER IMMEDIATELY for I am suffering tortures.   4286-1 Report File

In order to assist Sara with her problem, Cayce first outlined a series of physical measures, as her longstanding nerves and anxiety had apparently created problems within her physical body, making the situation even worse. She was advised that she needed to get away and learn to relax—the readings even recommended a sanitarium. Other recommendations included a change of diet and exercise, prayer, osteopathy, and aromatherapy, as a means of learning to relax.

Having had previous experiences in a sanitarium, Sara refused to go to another one. However, she thought a life reading outlining the karmic reasons for her fear might be helpful. Cayce agreed to help, stating, "for I assure you I want to be of help if possible. You are worth all the time and effort that I can possibly give, to get you set aright about this." The reading was acquired a short time thereafter and began describing Sara's most recent past life, as follows: "In the one before this we find in those days when the first settlers came into this land. The entity was then among those who gave in the development of those lands, and came among those first settlers . . . " (4286-3)

The reading went on to state that during that incarnation Sara had experienced the worst fate a mother could endure: she had been witness to all of her children being taken and apparently burned alive by those who were not happy with the arrival of settlers to the continent. The reading suggested that the experience had caused her to become wrathful with God for not protecting her children. The agony and torment of that experience had also caused her to vow never again to endure such personal pain. Apparently, the karmic memory of witnessing her children's death had caused her to be fearful of childbirth as a means of not having to ever again experience a similar loss. At long last, Sara had a rational explanation for her irrational fear.

The reading went on to suggest that, because of this horrendous experience, Sara often sabotaged herself and her own happiness, frequently preventing herself from obtaining goals or those things that she desired out of fear, that if they were obtained, they would simply be taken away from her. She was encouraged to redirect her energies (and her self-directed fear) into serving others. Although the particular kind of service was up to Sara, she was encouraged to help others who had lost their way to find their own relationship with the divine; in so doing she was assured that she would find her self. In the process, she would "bring joy, peace, comfort, to others, [and] pleasure to self." By following this approach, Sara could at last bring healing to the karmic memory that she had longed to heal within herself.

In addition to family relationships providing a means for the meeting of karmic memory within the self, the readings frequently pointed out examples of how various souls had been drawn back together in order to provide a helpful influence in terms of soul growth and personal transformation. For example, when Evelyn Carter asked Edgar Cayce about the past-life origin of her closeness to her granddaughter Donna, Cayce replied that it was simply a continuation of the relationship they had shared in Persia.

During that incarnation, Evelyn had been Donna's mother and the two had experienced a great deal of personal spiritual growth by their involvement in a movement that would eventually become the Zoroastrian religion. The helpfulness of that influence resided as a soul memory for both grandmother and granddaughter.

When Evelyn inquired as to how she could best assist and guide her granddaughter in the present, the reading explained that in various incarnations the girl had acquired the tendency to be somewhat lazy and was prone to putting things off or just doing enough to get by. Part of the reason that the two had been drawn back together was so that Evelyn could help her granddaughter overcome her laziness and re-awaken the spiritual longing that had once been a part of their joint soul history (1391-1 and 1401-1).

Because free will remains the strongest component in any relation-ship, however, a less-than-desirable outcome in the bringing of two souls back together can be seen in the example of a husband and wife that came to Edgar Cayce in 1942 and obtained life readings. During the course of the wife's reading, she asked how her husband might assist her in her career—she was an actress and he was a radio station man-ager. During the course of the husband's reading, he inquired about the karmic connections between them.

Cayce outlined a series of lifetimes for each of them—apparently the two had been together in a variety of relationships. Cayce also sug-gested that each possessed innate talents and faults that would impact their lives in the present. In the husband's case, he was a brilliant con-versationalist and had been trained in past-lives as a professional speaker; it was a talent he was encouraged to pick up in the present. In terms of his shortcomings, he was told that he had the tendency to lose control of himself and his anger far too easily. Conversely, the wife was informed that she had a flair for the dramatic arts and possessed an excellent singing and speaking voice. In terms of her shortcomings, she was prone to be critical of others, as well as moody and self-condemn-ing.

Their readings suggested that the lifetime having the greatest impact on them in the present came from a sojourn in ancient Rome. At the time, the husband had been a servant and speechwriter who pitied himself for his station in life. During that period the wife had been a man and a professional speaker and actor. Apparently the husband had served his present wife in something of a slave-master capacity and there existed some unresolved karmic memory between the two from that experience that needed to be worked through in the present. The reading counseled them: " . . . there are those things in the present to be met from that sojourn." (2706-1) When the husband inquired how they might constructively work on their karma, Cayce suggested that they work with the idea that ultimately "each is a complement to the other," even in terms of their careers. The wife was encouraged to allow her husband to assist her as an instructor in speaking and voice, much as he had done previously in Rome. When she asked what she could do to make her marriage a "lasting success," Cayce advised: "Know that it is a fifty–fifty proposition. Don't build it on 'What may I get?' but rather on 'What may I give?'" (2655-1)

Unfortunately, in spite of the fact that the couple was counseled about their past lives, their karmic connections and their respective strengths and weaknesses, they were unable to remain together and they eventually divorced. It's impossible to ascertain how much of the husband's temper or how much of the wife's critical nature led to the downfall of their marriage. What we can know for certain, however, is that whatever negative karmic memory remained or was created in their most recent life together will need to be worked through at some point in the future because life is a completely lawful experience.

Part of the lawfulness of life is the fact that there is a meaningful intent within the dynamic of every family relationship. To be sure, because of the nature of free will, each soul does not necessarily make the best use of that intent in terms of life choices. Ultimately, however, all families are drawn together for the purpose or with the intention of helping each individual become a better person. Sometimes that help might come through a positive relationship, such as a supportive spouse whose actions and nurturing guidance encourages her or his partner to become all that the individual was meant to be. Conversely, a negative relationship such as having a critical parent might enable the child to eradicate any similar patterns from within him or herself. With this in mind, even the most difficult relationship can ultimately be helpful in terms of soul growth and personal transformation.

Edgar Cayce believed that every aspect of family karma was simply the soul meeting itself. Throughout history all individuals have experienced both positive and negative relationships with every person in their families. Those relationships leave a residue of memory within the self—a memory that must be dealt with and transformed in the soul's ongoing process of evolving consciousness. It is not that individuals encounter family karma as a punishment, rather it is that they choose to work through that memory and heal it so that they can eventually learn to love everyone in the same manner that the Creator loves—unconditionally. Ultimately, what may be most astonishing about the Cayce information on family karma is what it suggests about the soul's deep connection to all other beings, the state of awareness that is the destiny of each and every soul, and the inevitability of the soul's ultimate relationship with the Creator.

2

Karmic Relationships with a Spouse

For, they are necessary one to the other in filling those purposes for which their activities are in this present experience.

As to application, this must be according to the choice of each. They should be cooperative, one with another.

The way ye know. The application ye must make. 849-60

ℰ

The Edgar Cayce readings suggest that souls are drawn together on account of their past-life connections and because they have the opportunity to learn from one another in the present. In terms of marriage, rather than presenting the idea that there is one perfect "soul mate" for each person, the readings suggest instead that individuals possess many soul mates. In fact, soul mate relationships can manifest between couples, between parents and children, between various family members, and between friends or even enemies. Actually, any individual with whom there is an intense emotional connection (positive or negative) is in all likelihood a soul mate with whom there is a relationship for mutual growth and development.[6] With this in mind, any marriage generally entails the coming together of "soul mates."

During the period that Cayce was giving readings, literally hundreds of couples sought and received relationship advice. There were individuals who came as a means of trying to gain insight or understanding as to why a certain situation had occurred in their marriage. Others sought counsel that could help them in experiencing a mutually beneficial relationship. On occasion there were those who inquired about marrying a specific individual. In the most difficult of situations, some looked for guidance as to the advisability of a separation or a divorce. Taken together, the Edgar Cayce information on marriage present basic recommendations for an ideal marriage, just as they contain guidance in terms of the rationale for divorce.

As far as recommendations for a helpful marriage, the readings suggest several principles that need to be at the heart of any mutually beneficially relationship: (1) marriage is a 50/50 proposition; (2) individuals in a marriage need to establish a "unity of purpose" (e.g., what are we trying to achieve in this relationship?); and, (3) selflessness rather than selfishness is necessary for both individuals. When a twenty-eight-year-old lawyer and his fiancée sought relationship guidance in order to achieve their "desires for matrimonial happiness and successful lives," Cayce gave the couple a definition of love—a love that would enable them to keep their marriage alive:

> Remember each, love is giving; it is a growth. It may be cultivated or it may be seared. That of selflessness on the part of each is necessary. Remember, the union of body, mind and spirit in such as marriage should ever be not for the desire of self but as *one*. Love grows; love endures; love forgiveth; love understands; love keeps those things rather as opportunities that to others would become hardships.
>
> Then, do not sit *still* and expect the other to do all the giving, nor all the forgiving; but make it rather as the unison and the purpose of each to be that which is a *complement* one to the other, ever.   939-1

Generally, when individuals sought help because of a difficult marital relationship, Edgar Cayce provided counsel that described the karmic memory that created the situation in the first place, as well as advice for working through and healing the problem in the present. Most often, the readings did not recommend divorce, as it was seen as simply a postponement of a lesson or a situation that would eventually need to be faced. However, there were occasions when divorce or separation was recommended. Individuals were advised to end their relationship if one of the following was occurring in their marriage: (1) if the individual was in physical, mental or spiritual danger by remaining with the other person; (2) when two people had come together and each had overcome what required to be worked out together; and, (3) when one individual had overcome the lesson and the other refused to. For example, on one occasion a fifty–three–year–old woman was encouraged to follow–through on a divorce and told: "thy usefulness one to another has passed." (3179-1)

In another instance, a forty–seven–year–old housewife was reassured that she had apparently met the karmic memory created in her most recent past life with her husband. In spite of the fact that the marriage had failed and was predicted to come to an end within the year, Cayce reassured her when she asked the question, "Has the karmic debt between us been paid during our 19 years of marriage?" He replied, "Been paid—and more." (1554-2) Connecting this meeting of self with her own soul growth, the reading added: "Then, the retardment or advancement of each soul—as this entity—depends upon how well it comprehends or applies its understanding."

Conversely, the case of a thirty–seven–year–old accountant named Jerry suggested that divorce was not yet an option as there was still more to learn. Jerry and his wife had been having problems and had even discussed the possibility of divorce. It was the second marriage for each of them, and a series of financial and emotional challenges had put them in a state of turmoil. Cayce suggested that in previous lives the two of them had encountered one another on numerous occasions, most recently in the eighteenth century. Then his present-day wife had been something of a bar moll and loose woman who often sought out "a good time." Jerry had apparently been a rancher that had left his wife to be with her. The couple was told that the feelings and problems they were experiencing in the present were simply the karmic response to their past relationship. Rather than thinking that their marriage had been a mistake, they were encouraged to know that is was, "*not* of chance but a purposeful experience for each . . . " Cayce went on to say:

> . . . each may be a helpmeet one to the other in attaining and gaining such an understanding of the purposes for that meeting, that association, as to *attain* the correct concept of the *purpose* of their incoming or entrance into this material experience.
> Know that this has not been completed in the present, and thus is to be *met in each!*
> Then why not now?   1650-2

In every instance, rather than seeing challenges in relationships as some kind of punishment, the readings instead suggest that these difficulties are simply the lawful meeting of individual memory within each individual. Cayce's advice to couples was to see self as being ultimately responsible and not the other individual as being the source of blame: "They each are faced with *themselves!* It is nothing but themselves they are faced with!" (1173-11)

Another very interesting example of karma is the case of Walter Youngston, a thirty-four-year-old attorney who sought relationship advice in the form of an Edgar Cayce life reading. Married to his wife, Susan, for ten years, about seven years into their marriage his wife had begun going out and having "clandestine" relationships with other men. Later, Walter began having an affair of his own with a woman named Frances, with whom he was now in love. When Susan found out about the affair, her response was to disavow any further affairs of her own and profess her "renewed love" for her husband. Walter's essential reason for having the reading was the following question: "Should I try to rebuild my married life with my present wife or separate from her and agree to a divorce . . . Should I then marry Frances . . . ?" The conflicting emotions Walter felt about the situation are evident in the fact that over the next 2½ years he would obtain three readings about the problem.

The first reading discussed the past-life experience most responsible for creating the karmic experience essentially as follows: During the period when the Israelites wandered the desert for 40 years, Walter had been a member of the tribe and once again the husband of Susan, his lawful wife. Rather than strictly following the laws of the Israelite community, however, Walter instead fell into lust with a "heathen" woman. As a result, he effectively "put away" his own wife, forsaking her to be with the other woman. Not only had he committed adultery, but the act of being with a non-Israelite woman was completely against the spiritual tradition of his people. It came as no karmic surprise to find that the woman with whom he had committed adultery had returned in the present as Frances.

In addition to describing the circumstances that had created the present-day situation, Cayce also chastised Walter for so frequently falling short of his own spiritual values and ideals throughout many of his lifetimes: "For, few records have we had here where there are greater possibilities, and few that have done less about their abilities in some of the experiences . . . Hence too often the entity has lost sight, and does lose sight of the purposes of a soul or entity entering a material experience." (2052-1) Later, the reading explained that the information was not simply trying to get him to be a "goody-goody, but good *for* something!" He was encouraged to work on his relationship with his wife, to go out of his way to purposefully do good, and to become a source of encouragement to others.

Less than three months later Walter had a second reading about the situation. He could not break off his attraction to Frances, nor could he bring himself to completely trust Susan. Cayce encouraged him to reconcile with his wife. The reading also suggested that some personal introspection might be helpful in determining that his wife was not solely responsible for their problems. The information made it clear, however, that Walter's course of action was a matter of free will. On a positive note, Walter was told that his relationship with Susan could become one in which they were truly happy together if the proper choices were made. His advice included the following:

This is a choice which must be made in self. There has been or may be felt within self that there are question marks as to the conduct of the companion. Art thou free from censure, thyself? How thinkest thou? Art thou more righteous than she?

There *are* those possibilities of this becoming a union in which *both* may become *real* helpmates one for the other. As to whether or not this is most desirable, must be a decision made twixt thee and thy companion! But analyze the purposes, the desires of each. Have you each learned your lesson? Are you each willing to leave *all else* and be one in purpose, in desire— which *is* the law of companionship of man and wife? Or will there be the demanding of the one, and the lack of sincerity on the part of the other?

. . . These are questions and answers as to same, that may be had only within thy own conscience—according to what has been and is thy ideal.   2052-2

The reading reminded Walter Youngston that the choice was up to him.

In spite of the readings' advice, for a time Walter went back and forth between both women. Finally, he got an illegal "quickie" divorce and married Frances. However, shortly thereafter he felt guilty and returned to Susan. Frances became upset and moved out of state, which was part of the impetus that prompted Walter to obtain his third and final reading. The primary question Walter asked was the following: "Considering that he seems to love them both in different ways and doesn't want to injure either one, you will advise the entity as to his choice between Susan . . . (in New York) and Frances . . . (in Ohio)."

The reading began by stating that the reason the situation was still a problem was because of Walter's predisposition to self-indulgence and self-gratification and that he found Frances physically "superior" to Susan, with whom he still had his primary obligation. He was strongly encouraged to discontinue his relationship with Frances, except as a means of perhaps helping her to find her next step in life. In terms of his relationship with Susan, he was told: "There needs to be the closer relationships with the entity whom *this* body, *this* entity so belittled in that experience . . . " (2052-3) Additional advice was given as to how to improve his relationship with his wife. When Walter again asked about the advisability of leaving Frances and the effect it would have upon her, the answer came: "better for *all* concerned."

When the reading was complete, Edgar Cayce's secretary, Gladys Davis, wrote a letter and sent it to Walter along with the copy of his reading:

Dear Mr. Youngston:

Your problem is a very interesting one from the standpoint of our research on the law of cause and effect, according to the laws governing reincarnation . . . You may not have understood fully the significance of your incarnation when you were the husband of Susan and forsook her for Frances . . . It was against the law of Moses for the Israelites to associate with women outside of their group. You, with many others, broke that law . . .

Naturally, you cannot in the present be free from Susan—you have an obligation which dates back to that period when you not only thought so little of her that you belittled her in the eyes of all the people by turning to a heathen woman, but you thought so little of the laws given to Moses by God that you broke them in such a way as to become a curse to many. Even if you got a divorce in the present, you would still be tied to Susan. When a spiritual law is broken, it must be met in the spiritual realm. When a material law is broken, it must be met in the material realm. In that sojourn you broke both the material and the spiritual law. Consequently, in the present you have the opportunity to meet it in both realms—by remaining true to your material vows not only in the flesh but in the spirit . . .

You asked if the Readings ever advise divorce. Yes, they do. In several instances a divorce has been advised, where the two people had either overcome what they had to work out together or else one had overcome and the other *would* not. But first every means has to be used to make things work. I notice from your letter some years ago you spoke of Susan going through a period of seeing other men clandestinely. Can't you understand, from the above, how that would be her natural inclination—if you were becoming cold with her? Not having been able to depend on you in that long ago period, no doubt she has felt many times the urge to defy you or to do something to hurt you . . . because of the hurt you did to her long ago. These thoughts and feelings do not die, but they live on and on within us, from age to age, until we have either become so degraded as to have no conscience or else so spiritual-minded as to become one in purpose with our Creator. The dependent love which Susan holds for you is exactly what you need—it is giving you the opportunity to make up for that other time . . . With Susan holding the proper attitude of love and protectiveness which you should holding the proper attitude of love and protectiveness which you should have, you could be happy—because you would know innately that you were doing the right thing, and you could make her happy. With your attitude changed, I am sure that you can find such happiness with Susan that you have never dreamed of . . .

I hope you will take this letter in the spirit with which it is sent. My desire was to clarify matters as I see them.

Sincerely, Gladys Davis, Secretary to Mr. Cayce

2052-3 Report File

In spite of the readings' advice, Walter went back and forth between the two women until each apparently abandoned him. Three years later, Walter wrote that he was then pursuing another relationship with a woman nearly twenty years his junior. That relationship eventually failed as well, and afterwards Walter sent another letter stating that he felt "lonely and emotionally devastated" and often wanted to simply give up on life. During the 1950s, Walter moved to Japan because of his job and wrote to A.R.E. requesting information, as well as copies of his own readings. After that request no further information on his subsequent relationships is on file; however, the lawfulness of karmic memory makes it clear that for his own growth and development Walter will inevitably have to face the situation with Susan and Frances at some point in the future.

The following example of karma in marriage presents a situation in which a couple was brought back together for the opportunity of meeting self, and the eventual outcome was that one apparently learned the necessary lesson and one apparently did not. During the course of a reading, a thirty-six-year-old woman was told that during a Grecian past life her husband had been her weakness in terms of getting her to sway from her spiritual and religious beliefs. In time, this had created a great deal of fear and doubt for her in that former experience. In the present, the fear and doubt had returned as she found herself with the same husband who was now an alcoholic. In describing why the woman had attracted the situation to her, the reading explained: "For each soul must meet *itself* and *its* activity *in the earth*; whether in a particular sojourn or in *whatever* the activity may be. For Life is *one*! And what ye sow ye *must* also reap." (845-1) Because of the workings of karmic memory, the same fear and doubt had to return and yet her response to that experience had to be very different in order to overcome it. In the present, she was encouraged to become the strength that her husband needed and yet this time she was not to sway from her own convictions or beliefs.

The woman returned for a follow-up reading more than one year later. On that occasion, Cayce told her that she was doing very well in providing strength for her husband, even in spite of the fact that he appeared to be making little progress in overcoming his addiction. When the woman asked about another relative with whom she was having difficulties and why these experiences kept coming into her life, the reading replied: "For each soul, each entity, constantly meets self. And if each soul would but understand, those hardships which are accredited much to others are caused most by self. Know that in those you are meeting thyself!" (845-4)

In terms of her relationship with her husband and her own personal development, she had made changes that the reading called "helpful"— changes that would enable her to be pulled down no longer by her connection to this soul. She had not swayed from her own convictions and beliefs. It was apparently for all of these reasons that the reading advised her that she could become an even greater help by seeking a divorce or separation—a move that would make him finally realize the extent of his problem.

The case of a thirty–four–year–old wife and mother contained in the Cayce files demonstrates how past–life behavioral patterns are frequently part of the karmic memory that impacts individuals' relationships in the present. During the course of her life reading, the woman learned the possible reason behind her husband's authoritarian nature and the dominant role he tried to play in their relationship. While reviewing the woman's past–life history, Cayce told her that her husband had once purchased her for two thousands pounds of tobacco during an early American incarnation. While giving the reading and discussing her interaction with her husband, Cayce asked her: "He bought you! Doesn't he act like it at times?" To which the woman responded: "He sure does!" (1222–1)

In a contemporary example of karmic servitude and role reversal, Mindy Larsen tells the story of being "emotionally imprisoned" by her verbally abusive, controlling, alcoholic husband for ten years. During that time her self–esteem was shattered and she saw her dream of what it would be like to be married to this one–time "love of her life" totally destroyed. One day, in the midst of her depression and despair she remembers asking God aloud: "Why? Why? Why is this happening to me?" Immediately, she saw a scene unfold before her eyes that seemed to come from her own long ago past:

> I was in a land of sand and hills—much like Saudi Arabia. I saw myself as the male leader of a tribe of nomads. Hard times had come. I suddenly knew that my present-day husband was then a woman in bondage and service to the tribe. All at once, I heard a voice say very clearly, "He was once your prisoner, now *you* are a prisoner of his love."

The experience helped Mindy understand the connection she had to her husband and enabled her to give up her "victim role" and instead take responsibility for her actions thereafter. She began working on for-giveness and detachment—finally being able to let go of "what could have been." She sought counseling, read, prayed, learned to meditate, and undertook a process she described as: "finding out about me, God, and what did I want." In the end, Mindy and her husband divorced but rather than holding any anger toward him, she is grateful for her new-found emotional and physical freedom:

> I am now free to grow. I am a better person. I am independent. I really look forward to being of service in some way—per-haps becoming involved with helping those who are victims of domestic abuse, or getting involved in hospice work, which I have done before. Meanwhile, I plan to simply enjoy my garden and each and every moment that God has given to me.

Another karmic role–reversal situation occurred in the case of Kitty Windsor and her husband, Peter. Married for twenty–one years, Kitty hadn't the slightest inkling that the two of them were on the verge of divorce. However, one day Kitty was shocked to discover that Peter was having an affair with a much younger woman:

> When I confronted him, he packed up and left without any discussion whatsoever. I was absolutely devastated. I couldn't believe my husband of twenty-one years could be so heartless and uncaring. I was devastated. I didn't believe I could ever forgive him or even attempt to make a new start in life as a fifty-year-old woman.

Her devastation led her to pursue a past–life regression as a means of coming to terms with the situation. According to Kitty, the regression coupled with her divorce ending up being "the turning point in my life—physically, mentally and spiritually." She describes witnessing her regression experience like a movie playing inside of her head:

> It was like being a witness to a movie—a movie of a past life

between Peter and myself. I saw a young couple, very much in love. His name was George; her name was Penelope. They lived in England during the 17th century and worked as servants in a large manor house. She was a house servant and he was a groomsman in the stables.

They had grown up together as servants in the manor house, and they had always loved one another. They loved to ride out together on horses and take picnics into the countryside to have under the trees. Eventually they married.

I saw a scene from later in their relationship. George was staring out the window toward the manor house—longing for something better than his station in life, and hoping to see the woman of the manor, whom he now dreamed of being with. Penelope was sitting in bed and crying because George had become so mean. She was pregnant and George found her ugly and misshapen, causing her to sink into a deep depression.

George's every thought was of the woman in the manor house—everything about her looked so much better than what he had. When it came time for Penelope to deliver the child, both she and the baby died during the birth process. George was sad, but he viewed it as his opportunity to finally get what he really wanted. To his surprise, the woman of the manor rebuffed him, for he was "only a groomsman."

In time, George realized that he had lost the only woman he had ever loved. He grieved so much that he literally drank himself into an early death. It was the shock of my life to understand that I had been George and Peter had been Penelope—karma strikes again.

Kitty then understood that the pain she was experiencing was the very same pain she had put her husband through in their English incarnation. It was that understanding that really enabled her to begin her own healing process. It was as if a light bulb had gone off inside her head and everything began to make sense to her. Kitty describes the experience as a "godsend." She was able to forgive her husband first and then herself second for having done essentially the same thing previously: "It felt like a weight lifted off my shoulders, and I began to trust that the universe would handle things rather than my being fearful and having to have control. I now believe that other people are put in our path for a reason, to work out problems, to rejoice in each other's company, but ultimately to help with each other with soul growth." Finally, Kitty says with a smile, "I still find it interesting that when my husband and I first began dating I gave him a plant, and for some inexplicable reason (at the time) he decided to name it George."

A more positive outcome for a relationship in which one individual was not entirely faithful is told in the contemporary story of Irene and Judy, a lesbian couple. The two have managed to stay together in spite of the cross-country distance between them and a problem that occurred early on in their relationship. Although the geographic distance has been challenging at times, their respective professional careers enable each of them to do quite a bit of traveling. "And so we try to see each other at least once a month," Judy says, "plus cell phones and daily conversations make the distance seem less of a problem."

The two were introduced by mutual friends during their respective travels and there was an instant attraction between them. According to Judy, "We dated for a while and finally decided to get together in spite of living on separate coasts. Although it might have seemed like an obstacle to other couples, it just seemed like we were supposed to be with each other."

After they became a couple, Judy realized it wasn't the geographic distance that would prove to be their biggest challenge; instead, it was Irene's difficulty remaining faithful in the relationship. "I was hurt and shocked when I found out what was happening," Judy admits. "I couldn't believe it, but at the same time I didn't want to lose her." One night, after a long-distance argument, Judy had a dream that seemed to explain how the two had ended up in their present situation:

> I seemed to be in New York at the turn of the 20th century. I was living in a brownstone with my husband, who I knew was Irene. Although much of our life together was rewarding

and we seemed to be happy, I found out my husband was cheating on me. Part of me felt shamed, but I couldn't bring myself to confront him about what was happening. I was very insecure and worried that I might lose him.

Upon awakening, Judy realized that the insecurity she felt in the dream was very much like the insecurity she had felt in relationships throughout her entire life: "I have a real fear of abandonment." At the same time, however, she realized that she had to do something to change the pattern. After much introspection, Judy realized that the only answer was to give Irene an ultimatum, even if it meant losing her: "I knew that Irene needed to overcome her pattern in relationships, just as I needed to overcome my personal insecurities and fears of being alone."

After Judy confronted her, Irene promised to change. The couple continued to work together, and in time they became even closer. The two picked up the positive memory of their connection with one another as well as the challenges they had faced in the past, using the first to overcome the second, and according to Judy, "We have never been happier."

Another contemporary account is the story of Helene Mayes, who not only describes a karmic connection between her and her husband, Brian, but also suggests that she was psychically connected to Brian long before they were ever married. Helene says she first "saw" Brian when she was an eleven-year-old during the Cuban missile crisis of the 1960s. In the midst of one of her daily "hide under your desk in case of attack bombing drills" she saw a sailor:

I "flashed" on an image of a sailor on a carrier. He had curly, auburn hair and was gazing out to the ocean. I later told my mom, "I hope we don't have a war because the man I am going to marry is on a ship out there." She told me that I had an over-active imagination. At the time, I figured he had to be about ten years older that I was.

Years passed and Helene essentially put the incident behind her. She met and fell in love with a man named Brian, who was ten years her senior. The incident was brought to mind, however, one day when they were packing books for their new home:

Shortly after we were married, we were going through a box of books and we came across his Navy yearbook from the *Essex*—the aircraft carrier he was on.

As I leafed through the pages, Brian said he had been stationed on the carrier during the Bay of Pigs incident. I finally came to a page that pictured a sailor with curly, auburn hair and a jaunty hat. I nearly fell over when I realized it was Brian. It was the same pose I had seen from the age of eleven. Brian told me he loved standing on the fantail of the ship and staring out to sea overlooking the ocean.

During her twenties, Helene had a dream that portrayed when she and Brian had last been together. Helene says that the dream was an "incredibly vivid experience" in which she saw herself as a member of the resistance or underground in France during World War II. In the dream, she was with a group of women meeting American soldiers at a bridge to exchange information they had about Nazi troop movements. Rather than simply being an exchange of information, apparently some of the women had developed relationships with the American soldiers, including herself. Helene knew that one of the soldiers was Brian. In the dream, she saw the women and soldiers come together on a bridge. All at once the Nazis opened fire in an ambush. Helene saw herself wounded, falling off the edge of the bridge into the black water below where she drowned. Approximately seven years later, the dream and her past–life connection to Brian was brought to mind when she saw the actual bridge in waking life:

Brian and I were driving home from France. At the time, he still worked for the service and I worked for American Express in Germany. We stopped for gas and decided to take the more scenic federal highway the rest of the way. Just outside of Saarbrucken we rounded a corner and there in front of us was THE BRIDGE! I had goosebumps all over. The only thing different was that a cement erosion control wall had been built along the hillside, but in every other detail it was the same.

Not only had Helene picked up a relationship with her boyfriend from the past but the two were able to visit the same spot in which they had last been together as a couple.

In another example of karma between spouses, Hannah Olsen is a seventy-five-year-old retired nurse who states that she has come to understand that her "hatred of Catholics, challenges with my husband, interest in metaphysics, and problems with my hip were all connected to the same past life." As a child, Hannah's upbringing led her to be sympathetic of all religions; however, she just couldn't bring herself to accept Catholicism: "I just felt like there was something about the religion I couldn't trust."

A nurse for much of her life, after a number of years of marriage, Hannah became interested in metaphysics, reincarnation, spiritual healing and Therapeutic Touch. At best, her husband didn't support her beliefs; at worst, he couldn't understand how she had gotten involved in such "nonsense." Oftentimes, rather than admit to attending a conference or doing something that she knew her husband would throw a fit about, she simply let him think that she was busy with work. The deception caused her mixed emotions: "I felt controlled and angry that he wouldn't support what I was interested in but at the same time I felt guilty for not being totally honest about what I was doing." It was somewhat ironic that the sciatica in her hip and leg acted up the most whenever she felt guilty about her activities.

When the day came that Hannah's son married a Catholic and converted to the religion himself, she felt the need to begin some serious introspection: "I had no earthly reason to feel about Catholics the way I did." When she prayed for understanding in terms of what she was supposed to do about the situation, it seemed as if a "still small voice" came into her head: "simply learn to love." Then one day Hannah had an experience that seemed to tie all of the pieces together:

I was attending a spiritual healing workshop in Philadelphia. Part of the program included a healing meditation. During the

> meditation, I felt my sciatica really begin to act up and I won-
> dered to myself, "Why is this happening now?"
>
> Suddenly, I saw myself in Ireland as some kind of prophet-
> ess or oracle. I was really popular with the Irish peasants who
> came to me for healing and various things. The local bishop
> was not at all pleased with my popularity—or, with what he
> saw, as competition with the Church. At first he sent a warn-
> ing for me to stop what I was doing. When that didn't work he
> sent someone to break my leg. As soon as I had the experi-
> ence, I knew that the bishop had returned as my husband and
> that my sciatica was connected to that same experience.

After the meditation, Hannah decided that, if she was able to forgive
her husband in the present, she could rectify any past-life anger that
had created the karmic situation between them in the first place. She
immediately began to look back over their marriage, "letting go of all of
the blame and resentment." She also went out of her way to cultivate a
relationship with her daughter-in-law who, Hannah says, "is now like a
daughter to me." Slowly, she found the bravery to tell her husband about
her interests and her metaphysical pursuits and, in time, although he
never accepted them as his own, he stopped complaining about her
interest in them: "He just learned to accept that this is who I am."

When asked why she thinks her karmic situation occurred in the
present, Hannah says simply, "It was an experience that helped me learn
forgiveness and loving those around me with unconditional love."

Eunice Midland was forty-seven years old when she contacted Edgar
Cayce for help. At her wits' end, she was convinced that she was "failing
in every way" in terms of her home and marriage. The mother of two
teenage daughters, more often than not her youngest child was disobedient and belligerent. Her marriage was also falling apart and appeared
to be coming to an end. Although she had known of her husband's
liaisons with other women over the years, his current affair appeared
much more serious, causing her to worry about her and the children's
future. Her request for help included the following information:

On October eighth I will have been married twenty-two years.

My husband has many excellent qualities and is generous to a fault. Physically I am nicely taken care of, but there are other conditions that cause me much concern and I hardly know what to do about them. I have two daughters, one sixteen and one fourteen years of age. For many years my husband has been interested in other women but never too seriously until now. This is one of the problems I am facing. I have only known about the other woman for a little more than two years, altho the affair has been going on for seven or eight years. My husband has done some very wonderful things for her—things that are done only for those one loves. When I first learned about it I thought I just wouldn't be able to endure it but God heard my prayers and came to my aid in a very wonderful way by removing the anguish entirely. I can't tell you how it was done, I just know that it is gone forever. Even though I am no longer hurt by his actions, I do not wish to stand in his way of happiness but I feel my first concern should be the children and what is best for them. My children seem to have very little respect or courtesy for me. I do not know what has brought about this attitude, it hurts and distresses me so much. Surely I must be at fault to be such a failure in every way . . . Maybe my vision and understanding is just too small. Maybe I haven't used wisely what God has given me. I seem confused about so many things. I just don't know what to do but with all my heart I desire to do the right thing.

3292-1 Background Information

While giving the reading, Cayce provided a framework for the family karma that had brought the individuals together in their present relationships. Keeping in mind that karma is individualized for each and every soul, the information Eunice received dealt with her karmic memory and what she was trying to learn. Obviously the tone of the information would be somewhat different had it been given from the perspective of her husband's karmic lessons or ever her children's.

Eunice was told that her challenges with her youngest daughter, who was fourteen at the time of the reading, had begun thousands of years ago in ancient Egypt. During that period, the fourteen-year-old was a grown woman with many children of her own and Eunice was a teacher and emissary whose life had included a variety of experiences beyond motherhood. Evidently, because of the women's different backgrounds and experiences, the two had found frequent occasion to disagree and argue. The frustration each held toward the other had manifested in the present with Eunice often lecturing to her daughter about "do's and don'ts" and the fourteen-year-old rebelling, even to the point of tantrums. Conversely, her relationship with the older daughter was much more positive. The reading stated that part of the reason was that the two had been very close during an incarnation in the Holy Land, and they had apparently both been involved in a similar work during the Egyptian lifetime.

Eunice asked how she might guide and train her daughters in right "thinking and living." Rather than falling into her old Egyptian role of lecturer and teacher, Cayce suggested a different approach: "Live it thyself. Preach it little. For, what ye are speaks so loud, others seldom hear what ye say . . . Then let thy life be a pattern that they may take as the light along the road . . . Ye have not applied the whole truth. Be not a preacher. Be ye 'doers of the word.' (3292-1)

When Eunice inquired as to why her husband had been unfaithful to her in the present, Cayce replied that she had been unfaithful to him during a lifetime they had shared as early settlers to the United States. The experience of an unfaithful wife had apparently caused him much anguish and sadness. Those same feelings now had to be experienced by Eunice in return. Cayce told her that she was: " . . . meeting much of those material experiences in this sojourn—as related to feelings, relationships, companionship . . . for ye are meeting *only* thyself."

Toward the end of her reading, Eunice asked if it was her fault that she was "failing in every way". The response came: "The entity is *not* failing. Do not condemn self. Condemning of self is as much an error as condemning others. Live thine own self. Leave the results with God . . . do not feel that ye have failed. Do not judge self. You have not failed *yet*. You only fail if you quit trying."

Apparently what was most important was how Eunice felt about herself and her relationship with her children. At the end of the reading she was advised to divorce her husband as soon as it was clear in the minds of everyone in the family that her daughters were to live with her.

In another contemporary example of karmic memory, Chelsea Jergen came to understand how an irrational fear she had once experienced as a teenager and her husband's tendency to treat her "somewhat fatherly" were both rooted in the same past life. Chelsea describes her situation, as follows:

> When I was eighteen I was in a field on my grandparents' farm, enjoying a beautiful day. Suddenly, on the horizon I saw three people on horseback riding in my direction. I don't know why but all at once I panicked. For some unknown reason, I ran like my life depended on it. I have never been so frightened in my life. I ran until I reached my grandparents' house. When I got there, I hid behind the sofa until I was certain that I was safe—silly behavior for an eighteen-year-old but I was terrified.
>
> I never forgot the incident, or the feeling of panic, and I often wondered why I had acted that way. It's also interesting to me that this experience occurred shortly before I met the man who would become my husband.

Years passed, during which Chelsea married and had three children. In spite of the fact that she and her husband were only a couple of years apart, one of their relationship dynamics was the fact that her husband often had the tendency of treating her like she was one of the children rather than being his wife. It came across in the way he spoke to her, as well as the way he sometimes responded to some of her ideas or opinions: "At the very least, it made me frustrated and on a number of occasions I found myself saying to him, 'You are not my father.'"

At the age of thirty, Chelsea went to see a psychic with a friend of hers. She was determined not to tell the psychic anything beforehand and adds: "And I hadn't thought about the incident at my grandparents in a very long time." Almost immediately, the psychic began telling her about a recent past life in Turkey—the story tied together her fear as well as the way her husband spoke to her:

> According to this woman, I had been the daughter of a wealthy family in Turkey. One day I had been out playing when I had wandered a bit too far away. Suddenly, three riders on horseback came along and kidnapped me. I was used as a slave until I was a little older and ended up being won in a card game by a much older man—the man who is now my husband. She told me that he was kind and that we had married and he had reunited me with my family.

Needless to say, the psychic encounter helped Chelsea understand both her teenage fear, as well as her husband's response to her. She ended up telling her husband about the session with the psychic and worked with him until his "somewhat fatherly approach" was no longer an issue.

Contrary to the idea of having to fulfill relationship karma by coming back together as husband and wife, a thirty-three-year-old woman was told that she and her present-day boyfriend—with whom she was having difficulties—had been together at least three times previously. When she asked whether or not they should get married for their "mutual development," Cayce replied that there were definitely things that needed to be worked out in order to "meet" their karmic memory. Apparently, they had experienced a number of lifetimes when they had a hard time agreeing and working with one another cooperatively. It was that situation that needed to be healed. The karmic memory could be addressed as husband and wife, however, the reading tried to counsel her by stating: "But as husband and wife would be a hard way to meet same!" (2582-3) In other words, it might be easier to work through their karma in their present relationship dynamic and not by coming together as spouses.

Another example that explores karmic memory and divorce as the end result is the story of fifty-year-old Fran Wayman, who had been

divorced from her husband, Tom, for more than a decade. According to
Fran, Tom was domineering and abusive to both her and their children:
"He was the most controlling, anger–filled individual I have ever met.
He was prone to emotional outbursts and was extremely verbally abu-
sive and eventually physically abusive."

After a dozen years of marriage, Fran's situation deteriorated to the
point where she finally filed for a divorce. That same year she had a
hypnotic regression that convinced her the abusive relationship with
Tom had simply been a holdover from their most recent past life. Fran
describes the regression:

> I saw myself barefoot, wearing a tattered homemade dress and
> living in a very small, windowless, one-room cabin. I had a
> couple of children and I knew that my husband had been away
> for an extended period. While he was gone, a few times a
> friend of his had come to check on us, just to make certain we
> were okay. During one of these brief visits, my husband came
> home and saw his friend there.
>
> In spite of the fact that nothing had happened, my husband
> went into a jealous rage and began screaming—his friend sim-
> ply left. I tried to explain that nothing had happened and that
> his friend had done nothing to betray his trust but my hus-
> band was uncontrollable and accused the two of us of having
> sex while he had been away.
>
> My husband took hold of me and dragged me out into our
> fields with a bullwhip and repeatedly beat me. Whether it was
> intentional or not, I ended up dying. I remember hating him
> the whole time he was hitting me. Later, he went to his friend's
> and stabbed him in the back.
>
> After the death of the two of us, my husband realized that
> he could not continue working to support himself and care for
> his own children. Therefore, he loaded them up in a wagon
> and took them quite a distance—eventually selling them into
> indentured servitude.
>
> During this experience, I realized that the man who had

killed us both was my husband, Tom. I also knew that the friend he had killed had returned as our present-day son. Amazingly, our son was born with a scar on his back that exactly looks like a stab wound would look if it had not been stitched up.

Fran's regression made complete sense to her. First of all, the anger she saw portrayed in the experience was parallel to Tom's uncontrollable anger. In addition, her husband's relationship with his own children had always been somewhat distant and Fran realized that in addition to their son having been killed in the past by his own father, one of the children in the wagon had returned as the couple's present-day daughter. She realized that the relationship each of them shared with her ex was simply a continuation of feelings from the past. Although Fran has remarried and now lives with "a wonderful partner," she admits she still has to deal with Tom on occasion and he is still able to make her angry—it is something she has vowed to overcome:

> I know I still struggle with total forgiveness of this man, and yet I know it is something I need to do. He can still spark anger in me—whether it is over the unfairness of his prior actions, or even in the treatment of his grown children. I have to take a deep breath and remind myself that I must overcome this—or face yet another opportunity to work through it with this soul.

Another case illustrating the dynamics between divorce and the fulfillment of personal karma can be seen in the example of Doris Iverson, a forty-nine-year-old housewife at the time of her Edgar Cayce reading in 1943. Doris had a tremendous desire to work with children, especially young girls, but her husband (with whom she was having problems) was apparently against the idea of her having an independent career. Her reading confirmed her desire of working with children, stating it had also been her occupation throughout a number of previous incarnations.

According to the Cayce information, Doris had once helped couples establish their homes and prepare for the care of young children in a previous sojourn in ancient Egypt. During the formation of the early Christian Church, she had served in the role of a Mother Superior, seemingly attending to the needs of unwed mothers and their children. In Colonial America she had cared for her own family and still found the time to take in the children of other settlers, as well: "The entity was a homemaker—yes, with quite a family of its own; then in the name Geanet Hardcastle, the entity kept the children of others that were busy with the activities of the early settlers . . . the entity gained and almost determined to ever give itself in such activities." (3379-2)

It was also during the colonial period that she and her present husband had most recently been together. Apparently, at the time, he had not at all been happy about the presence of so many children in their household. The resulting karmic memory was that her husband did not want her to pursue her interest with children in the present.

Cayce told Doris that in their colonial marriage they had got along much better after they had separated and that she might wish to pursue the same course of action today: " . . . when you got rid of him you got along much better, you may do the same today." The rationale she was given was as follows:

> For the entity innately and manifestedly is a leader, a teacher, and an instructor for the young. Here it would be well not to allow the idiosyncrasies of one person—even though it is called the husband—to prevent the entity from fulfilling those abilities that are a part of the manner in which the entity may fulfil those purposes for which it entered this sojourn . . .
>
> Yes, it is well for the entity to be wedded—this is the natural life of an individual entity in the earth. But when there are those relationships that prevent the fulfilling of the purposes for which the entity entered, and these become apparent and there is no altering, it is better that there be dis-associations of such; that each may fall in that category through and in which they each may serve the God they have chosen in a life experience.   3379-2

On the other hand, Edgar Cayce told another couple not to divorce or separate in spite of their difficulties as each apparently needed the other in fulfilling their purpose in life and becoming better people. The reading told the two that they had been together on a number of occasions, including Jamestown, Rome and Persia. Some of their challenges seemed to be connected to the Roman experience when the wife had been in a position of nobility and her present husband had been drawn to her power but also repelled by her aloofness, as she held herself apart as a member of the upper class. Cayce advised the couple it was "not well to separate." (280-1) Instead they were encouraged to stay together. The wife was encouraged to become a leavening influence, using kindness, gentleness and a quiet manner to calm his rash nature and emotional outbursts. She was also encouraged to pursue her spiritual interests, cultivating her own intuitive abilities and, in turn, the understanding of how she could help bring health and happiness into their household. Five years after the reading the husband passed away, and when the wife gave a follow-up report more than ten years later on her experience with the Cayce information, this is what she had to say, in part:

> Yes, I still have a copy of my life reading. I have read it over eleven or twelve times, mostly with friends . . . My life reading is a solace to me, as these past-lives are proving a protection and a guidance, and an incentive to develop or grow in spiritual truth . . .
>
> We make our own karma, good or bad. As a result of my life reading, I have found peace and harmony through prayer and meditation, and the ability to help others to find themselves, in their trials and temptations, by holding to the ideal in the Creative Forces.   268-3 Report File

In a contemporary example of working through a karmic situation with a spouse, a woman learned from a psychic reading that the "competitive" relationship she had with her husband was directly connected to a time when the two had been neighboring nomadic leaders. Apparently, she had been less structured and more beloved by her people, while he had been extremely controlling, severe and yet more successful in making certain that the tribe had what it needed to survive. Their respective attitudes had continued into the present in terms of their relationship with their children. The woman also learned that his "air of superiority" was a holdover from that period, as well. Since he was open to the idea of reincarnation, the woman discussed the information with her husband and eventually the two agreed there appeared to be definite "patterns" that had resurfaced in the present—patterns that the psychic had identified without knowing the couple personally.

Because of the information, the woman became more understanding of her husband when she saw him fall into habitual responses, and her husband tried to become more aware of how he was coming across and treating members of his family: "Like a tribal leader who knows what's best for everyone," a tendency he had still fallen into from time to time. However, the couple has essentially worked through the former problems in their relationship. Today, the wife says: "Sometimes, I still see remnants of his former attitude but he is doing much, much better. I'm glad we stuck it out. We've become partners in life and I've gained a husband who is extremely devoted."

Miscellaneous examples of karma between spouses that can be gleaned from the Edgar Cayce material also include the following:

A husband and wife who apparently had a hard time cooperating with one another as well as difficulty treating each other as equals were told that this karmic challenge could be traced to two previous past-lives. In their most recent past life, she had been a male and her husband had been her employer. Previous to that, she had been of royalty in Egypt and her present-day husband had been a eunuch manservant that served under her rule. When asking for advice, the husband was told: "In thine seeking, in thine understanding, make that thou savorest of self do no more than that required of thine neighbor. Be tolerant . . . keep thine own body, thine own mind, thine own soul, in readiness to serve where the Master leads." (473-1)

Another couple learned that the tendency each possessed toward low self-esteem and belittling behaviors arose from an ancient Egyptian incarnation when the two had also been together. At that time they had jointly shared a position of leadership but the two had been frequently doubted and questioned in terms of their motives and leadership abilities. That questioning had led to the questioning of self—a trait that continued into the present. The wife was encouraged to overcome her karmic memory by ministering, teaching or communicating spiritual truths to others through the written word, whereas the husband was encouraged to use his position as an executive to inspire and motivate his employees (1315-2 and 437-2).

On another occasion, a woman inquiring about the karmic connection between herself and her demanding husband was told that their present-day experience was the result of at least two previous experiences. In one of her past lives she had been a kind of seer and prophetess who had men waiting on her hand and foot. In an even earlier incarnation in the Gobi, she had been a leader and teacher who directed the affairs of many. In both of those experiences her husband had been her servant. In the language of the readings: "For ever has the husband been as the servant—as thou servest now!" (1580-1)

Another woman, whose husband's career as a naval lieutenant often "ran her ragged," was told that in her most recent lifetime she was instrumental in preparing ships for sea. In inquiring about the karmic connection to her husband, she was told it had most notably been from that period: "In the experience before this—you ran him ragged for a while, and then settled down . . . in the present the experience is almost reversed but ye will keep the faith together. Ye have much to work out together." (3047-1)

In terms of building positive relationships with a spouse, the Edgar Cayce information offers a wealth of advice that is not only invaluable at building for the future, but also as a means of overcoming negative karmic memory from the past. For example, on one occasion when a twenty-year-old woman inquired whether her marriage to her fiancé would result in a "spiritual, mental and physical union," Cayce replied that it would become such if the two simply chose to make it so. In terms of how to bring it about, the advice was as follows: "Not continually seeking or finding fault, either one with the other—but correcting the errors, the faults, the shortcomings in *self*; and ye will bring the best that is in self and make for the manifesting of the best that is in thy helpmate." (1722-1)

Similarly, when a thirty-four-year-old business manager asked about his relationship with his wife and wanted additional information as to how they could meet their karmic memory, the reading promised that as they worked together with a common ideal they could become "a complement to the other." Cayce stated that, in spite of their attempting to work together, because of the nature of relationships there would definitely be "periods of disturbance." In order to meet those challenges, part of his advice was to "not both get angry at the same time." He also recommended the following:

> Let the ideals and the principals of each be one. Their manner of approach, their manner of thought need not necessarily be the same, but the purpose, the desire, the hopes, the welfare of each should be as is indicated in such a union, one for the other. Each should be ever mindful as to the welfare of that as may be for the glorifying of the truth, beauty, love, hope, self-sacrifice in their relationships not only to one another but to their problems, their joys, their sorrows, their blessings, their downsittings. All of these, let them be with that attitude as of a helpmeet one to the other.   341-48

Finally, when a twenty-three-year-old woman obtained a reading on her impending marriage and asked for advice on how she might adjust to her new life and establish a happy home, she was encouraged to pattern it after what she might surmise was a "heavenly home." The information she received portrays the ideal relationship environment that is depicted within the Edgar Cayce readings:

> Not as that set aside for only a place to sleep or to rest, but where not only self but all who enter there may feel, may experience, by the very vibrations that are set up by each in the sacredness of the home, a helpfulness, a hopefulness in the air

about the home. As not only a place of rest, not only a place of recreation for the mind, not only a place as a haven for the bodies and minds of both but for all that may be as visitors or as guests. And remember those injunctions that have been in thine experience in many of thine sojourns, and be thou mindful of the entertaining of the guests; for some have entertained angels unawares. Make thine home, thine abode, where an angel would desire to visit, where an angel would seek to be a guest. For it will bring the greater blessings, the greater glories, the greater contentment, the greater satisfaction; the glorious harmony of adjusting thyself and thy relationships one with another in making same ever harmonious. Do not begin with, "We will do it tomorrow—we will begin next week—we will make for such next year." Let that thou sowest in thy relationships day by day be the seeds of truth, of hope, that as they grow to fruition in thy relationships, as the days and the months and the years that are to come go by, they will grow into that garden of beauty that makes indeed for the home.

480-20

3

Karmic Relationships Between Children and Parents

Q. For what purpose did I choose my present parents in this incarnation?
A. For thine own enlightenment, and thy parents' understanding.   2632-1

Regardless of how individuals may feel about their families, the Edgar Cayce information suggests that part of the lawfulness of karma entails drawing specific individuals to one another, providing the opportunity for souls to learn specific lessons along the way. Stated more simply, people choose their parents. Although this concept of choice may make sense to individuals who were brought up with loving parents or raised in a supportive home environment, the idea may be somewhat challenging for those with extremely difficult upbringings or even with parents who were cruel and abusive. Why would a child choose to be born into such an environment? Why would individuals choose parents who didn't nurture and love them? In all likelihood, the answer is that no thinking human being would ever choose such a situation. However, that choice is not made at the level of human consciousness, it is made at the level of the soul.

From Cayce's perspective the soul is a spiritual being that, while in the earth, is having a physical experience. The seven to ten decades in human consciousness experienced at the level of personality are a mere flicker of an instant when balanced against the eternality of the soul. In the same manner that individuals will commit to a short period of intense training or an aggressive and demanding educational experience (like boot camp or medical school) in order to experience the rewards that lay beyond, the soul picks specific experiences in order to learn lessons important to the individual's personal growth and development.

With this in mind, a soul that has a problem with a rash and explosive temper might pick a parent with the very same problem as a means of eradicating it from the self. Conversely, an individual with a soul mission of helping vulnerable children could choose to be born into an abusive situation in order to be able to relate to the very same individuals that he or she would eventually try to help. Another possibility is that sometimes individuals get to personally encounter the same things they once imposed upon another. To be sure, people can also chose parents and family members with whom they have been close, and who have been extremely helpful in previous incarnations—picking up exactly where they left off. The case histories for the individuals who came to Edgar Cayce for assistance corroborate each of these situations, and others, as being genuine workings of karmic memory through the process of reincarnating into the earth.

Cayce biographer, Thomas Sugrue, both knew Edgar Cayce and for a time lived in the Cayce home. During the process of writing the biography, *There Is a River*, Sugrue obtained a reading and asked a couple of questions about children choosing to be born into the earth. He planned to use the information that he obtained by weaving it into the "Philosophy" chapter of *There Is a River*. One of Sugrue's questions was: "Does the incoming soul take on some of the parents' karma?" Cayce responded, "Because of its relative relationship to same, yes. Otherwise, no." (5749-14) The answer suggests that the "parents' karma" was only taken on by the incoming soul if it had been personally involved in the situation that had created the karma in the first place. In this instance, the karmic memory would belong to the child as much as it belonged to the parents.

Another question asked by Sugrue was, "Are there several patterns which a soul might take on, depending on what phase of development it wished to work upon—i.e., could a soul choose to be one of several personalities, any of which would fit its individuality?" Cayce's response was simply, "Correct," suggesting that there is much more to the soul than is manifested by the personality and that the soul is often involved in choosing what lessons it hopes to work with at any moment in time.

Oftentimes, individuals only briefly inquired about present-day family relationships. In those instances, rather than outlining detailed biographical sketches of the past, the readings simply presented brief explanations of the karmic memory experienced in the present. Some of these examples of the karmic connection between children and their parents are as follows:

On one occasion, a middle-aged woman wanted to know why her father had been such a source of antagonism for her. Cayce responded that it was simply the meeting of self: "For thou also antagonized him." (1183-1)

A mother and daughter who were frequently at odds with one another were told that the issue between them was one of control. The two had apparently switched past-life roles in that the daughter had once been her mother's mother. Cayce explained, "Thus often the questioning as to who shall be boss." (2969-2)

Actually, the switching of parental-child roles seems to be a frequent karmic response throughout many of the case histories contained in the Cayce files. For example, a seventy-two-year-old woman thinking of retirement and living with her daughter was encouraged to do so, just as her daughter had once lived with her when "conditions were reversed." (851-2) On another occasion, a thirty-one-year-old woman discovered that her three-year-old son had once been her father. At the time he had attempted to control and direct her. Part of the reason the youth had chosen her to be his mother was in an effort to have her help him "temper" this tendency (1294-1). A forty-nine-year-old woman learned that her present-day son had once been essentially her adoptive father: "Hence as ye will find, so oft thy present son would tell thee what to do!" (3576-1) When a sixty-nine-year-old farmer inquired about the karmic relationship he had experienced with his son, Cayce responded: "In the experience before this he gave you a good licking once, as ye have given him several this time! These are still innate things that must be worked out. Ye have come together for good. Don't lose patience with yourself nor with thy son." (2051-5) These are just a few of the many examples of role reversal from the readings.

When a thirty-two-year-old woman asked the reason that she and her mother were related in the present, Cayce explained that the two were reversing the roles they had lived in a French incarnation. Rather than seeing her relationship with her mother as an obligation or a duty, she was encouraged to see it as an "opportunity" to correct what had once gone wrong. The readings suggested that there was a still a purpose for them to work together:

> Where individuals come together in such an association, *ever* there is something to be worked out. For one has been or is dependent upon the other for some expression or some means or manner of reaching a development or an attunement to the Creative Forces in the experiences of each.   1695-1

Another woman was told that the two seemingly different relationships she possessed with her daughter were connected to two experiences from the past that had each created their own karmic memory. In one experience the daughter had been a one-time friend who eventually turned away from the friendship. It was from that experience that doubt and resentment often arose. In another lifetime, her present-day daughter had been her daughter then. From that lifetime there was the urge for the daughter to turn to her mother for counsel and advice, just as she had done in that previous incarnation. (2620-2)

These types of examples briefly describing the karmic connections between parents and children are contained throughout the Edgar Cayce life readings. There are also detailed case histories that present fascinating glimpses into how karmic memory works and how it sometimes involves every member of the family. The story of Franklin

Wagner, his wife Julia, and their daughter Debbie is one such example:
  Debbie Wagner was twelve years old when the family came to Edgar
Cayce for help. The girl was prone to epileptic fits, and family friends
had referred the parents for a reading. Debbie's condition had caused
her parents much concern, and previously they had sought out quite a
number of medical professionals to assist their daughter.
  Cayce gave a physical reading that outlined a series of treatments
that Franklin and Julia were encouraged to follow. The couple also received life readings that got to the heart of their present situation, as
well as the karmic memory involved. During the American Revolution,
Franklin and Julia had been married. At the time, the couple believed in
the sanctity of the British Crown and they were horrified with the idea
that the colonies were trying to gain independence. As a result, they
coerced their grown daughter into spying for England. During that incarnation, the girl was both attractive and had a highly developed sense
of intuition—apparently, both her body and her psychic abilities had
been used in service to the Crown. The couple was told that this daughter had reincarnated as Debbie in the present.
  Because the couple had used their daughter for their own selfish
purposes, much of their life in the present was spent trying to get help
for the girl. Because Debbie had once controlled others with her physical charms as well as her intuitive talents, the epileptic fits had come as
a means of making her lose control in the present. It was through the
family relationship that each individual was being given the opportunity to heal what had once gone awry. In the language of the readings,
"each soul must meet its own self" (2345-1) In an effort to clarify the
information and the karmic connection between the three, Hugh Lynn
Cayce (Edgar Cayce's eldest son) sent a letter to Franklin, explaining the
situation as follows:

> Your daughter's life reading indicates that a [karmic] debt was
> the basic cause of her physical condition at this time . . .
>   As I understand the picture, in the incarnation just before
> this, during the period of the American Revolution, you and
> your wife had a child, this same girl who is your daughter

today. At that time you believed in and worked for a British cause. You were instrumental in encouraging and perhaps forcing your daughter to act as a spy in securing information which could be used against the colonies. This in itself need not have been necessarily wrong, but evidently the methods employed broke the spiritual law in that they destroyed the ideals of the girl. I call your attention to the reference in your daughter's readings on page two, "as to relationship which excited the fires of physical beings of many."

Evidently your daughter was then possessed of some psychic ability which was misused . . . Evidently you attempted to force the girl to use the psychic ability, which you did not understand, to control others and to secure information which you desired. In your own reading we find the reference to "periods of confusion brought on by these attempt to gather data and information for use of those the entity felt were in authority." (Evidently referring here to the British authority.)

It is interesting to note that all psychic abilities involve the ductless glands of the body. The pineal, the pituitary, the thyroid and the adrenal as well as glands of reproduction are all connected in the expression of any psychic faculty. The fact that your daughter misused such ability in a previous incarnation brings over into the present the tendency, directed through the soul-mind, for a disturbance in the glandular system. Such glandular disturbances involve the type of trouble associated with your daughter's case.

You and your wife have the opportunity and the responsibility of helping this soul meet and overcome this condition. The fact that you have taken this responsibility indicates your own spiritual understanding and development. It is important that you help this child balance her life and express the finer characteristics and abilities. Understanding this relationship will be of great help in guiding and directing her life . . .

2345-1 Report File

According to notes on file, Franklin Wagner was extremely impressed with the information. Not only did it give him a recommended treatment to assist his daughter but it also provided a karmic explanation for their experience. Mr. Wagner remained an enthusiast of the Cayce work for years. In fact, when Edgar Cayce died, he sent Cayce's wife Gertrude the following letter of sympathy:

February 13, 1945
My dear Mrs. Cayce:
Upon my return to my office today after an absence of several weeks I was deeply grieved to learn of Edgar's untimely death. I had heard that he was indisposed, but I hadn't the slightest idea that his illness was so serious.

I can well understand what Edgar's death must mean to you and the boys; the loss of a devoted husband and loving father is indeed a grievous one. Always considering Edgar a God-fearing man and deeply admiring his saintly character, I deemed it a privilege to call myself his friend. Although, my acquaintance with Edgar was comparatively brief, he made a profound impression upon me, and since his death has effected me so much I can realize what it must mean to you, your family and Edgar's close associates. I am sure you understand Mrs. Cayce, how deeply I sympathize with you in your bereavement . . .

Inasmuch as the Association files are crammed full with his readings, and as I know that these contain invaluable advice and counsel on many important subjects, I do hope that you and the members of the Association will, to the fullest possible extent, make them available to those who, like myself, had such confidence in his judgement.
With sincere best wishes to you and the boys, I am
Faithfully yours, Franklin Wagner

Another case from the Cayce files exploring how present-day physical problems can be connected to karmic memory is the story of a twenty-seven-year-old man who had suffered with a "delicate" digestive system for his entire life. Even as a child, he had to have a diet carefully monitored by his mother. According to notations on file later written by his sister:

> For instance, he never could eat much cornbread—the rough-ness upset his stomach. If he ate as much sweets as the other children in the family he would become nauseated and vomit; he could never indulge in rich foods and get away with it as the rest of us did. Many times during his early childhood, I remember, he fell down—stumping his toe on a root or some-thing—and lost consciousness; seeming to indicate, with my later knowledge of the lacteal ducts, etc., that the digestive system was the cause of the fainting or loss of consciousness when he had a physical shock such as falling down.
>
> 641-1 Report File

During a life reading, the poor digestion was traced to lifetimes in both France and Persia when he had been a member of the courts and frequently prone to the excess of gluttony. The digestive problem was simply a way of enabling his soul to learn moderation. The individual's mother also had experiences in the French and Persian courts but it was a lifetime in Atlantis that proved especially helpful in the present. The two had been associated during that period when the mother had served in the role of dietician for the high priests. That same skill emerged in the present as her interest in health foods, as well as her ability to help her son with his digestive problem. The problem had once been so serious that one file notation reads: "If he had not had the good karma of such a mother he might never have lived to grow up, because such care was necessary in his diet during his early years." (641-6 and 1187-2)

Another exploration of karmic memory in the parent–child relation-ship is detailed in the story of Edith Maxwell, who had a series of read-ings from Edgar Cayce. Lonely throughout much of her life, eventually a reading described Edith's loneliness as a karmic situation because she had once abandoned two children. Although Edith had already obtained life readings as well as a reading for a physical condition, her sixth reading requesting additional details of a life during the early nineteenth century revealed the cause of her loneliness.

Besides providing the information that Edith asked for, Cayce proceeded to tell her about another lifetime that was the cause of her karmic loneliness. Apparently she had not been ready to hear the information earlier. Cayce explained that in the year 1592, during an incarnation in Norway, she had committed suicide. That event was at the heart of her carrying a "great loneliness" throughout much of her life.

Gina Cerminara, Ph.D., longtime scholar of the Cayce information and author of numerous books once described Edith's background as follows:

> . . . [her] first husband died shortly after marriage. She married again—this time to a man much older than herself, and the marriage was so unhappy that she soon obtained a divorce. She had no children. All the members of her family had died; she literally had no one. Her position as social secretary brought her into contact with people, but it was a superficial contact. She would have liked to remarry, but the opportunity did not present itself. She was alone. Cerminara, pg. 132

During the Norwegian lifetime, Edith's husband had apparently disgraced the family when he abandoned his religious beliefs. The end result was that Edith and her husband became outcasts in the community. Already the mother of one child, after the birth of her second child, Edith's sixteenth century counterpart decided she could take the exile no longer and she killed herself by throwing herself in a fjord. According to Cayce, this selfish act and the loneliness that Edith had caused for both her husband and two young children had to be met in the present in the form of karmic memory. The reading suggested that her present-day loneliness was simply the means in which she was meeting herself: "Thus we find the influences arising in the experience of the entity in the present—as the periods of what may be called melancholia, disappointments, discouragements." (1468-6)

Cayce went on to tell her that the husband she had divorced in the present was the same husband she had abandoned in Norway through her suicide. The two children she had left behind had also returned in her present incarnation: one had been her brother who had died, and the other was a friend that was described as being close one minute and distant the next. Cayce went on to assure her that the reason the information was being provided was that she had indeed grown spiritually and he pointed out that the growth had enabled her loneliness to diminish. He ended the reading by encouraging her to continue with her own soul growth and discovering her relationship to the Creator:

> For, as the entity continues to look within, there the promise has been and is that He, the way, the truth, the light, will meet thee; in making and bringing that into the experience, mentally, materially, that is the helpful force for the greater spiritual development.   1468-6

A contemporary example of karma in the parent–child relationship is presented in the story of Mark Cavanaugh. For a long while, Mark worked on trying to improve his relationship with his mother. More than anything, he wanted his mother to be nicer to him, and he did things to seek her approval—even trying to be someone that he really wasn't. He tried to be the son that he thought she wanted. He attempted to overcome his feelings of not being good enough. Even though he never recalls having a mother–son connection with her, he really wanted her to care. He knew that at one level she loved him but he really wanted to feel that love. He knows now that he was trying to get her to be someone other than who she really was.

When Mark was in his thirties, he had a dream that perfectly explained the karmic origins of their present-day relationship:

> I dreamt that she was a Roman woman of wealth and power, and I was her slave—a Christian slave. In that lifetime she abused me physically, verbally, and sexually—it is interest to note that even now, as an adult, I don't like her touching me affectionately. In that life, my mother was angry and critical. I

was a Christian and tried to follow Christ's teachings in order to get her to change her behavior towards me.

At one point, I snapped, realizing that she was never going to change, and I was going to be receiving her abusive treatment forever. My resolve and my mind broke, thinking that the abuse was never going to end. I broke her neck, and I was later killed by a Roman soldier for the crime.

During the dream, I saw myself after death and heard the voice of what I thought to be God say, "This is YOUR mother," meaning she was going to be my mother in a future life.

I was horrified. "She is not MY mother!" I replied.

Suddenly, I saw myself standing before Jesus. Although he looked upon me without judgment, He said: "It would have taken you this long to work things out with her." During his statement, He held his hands about six inches apart. Then he widened the gap between his hands to be at least double and added: "Now it's going to take this long."

The dream ended and I awoke.

After the dream, Mark understood that he still had a lot of work to do on his relationship with his mother. The tremendous attitude of being nonjudgmental that Jesus had shown him proved to be extremely helpful in healing his own attitude. He was able to let go of the need to have her change. He began to be comfortable with himself when he was around her, turning loose of the need to be someone else in order to win her approval. In time, he was able to accept her just the way she was. Because of his efforts, Mark is certain that the karmic situation between them has been healed. In fact, when asked if there is anything he would like to tell his mother at this point in time, Mark replies in the affirmative: "Thank you for being willing to be my mother. Thank you for trying to give me what you feel you were able to. Thank you for teaching me what you had to teach. May God continue to be with you on your journey."

Another contemporary account is told by Judith Beatty in describing a karmic situation with her son that seemed to foster healing on several levels. Now in her seventies, Judith can remember exactly how she felt the day after giving birth to her youngest child, Arnold, when the doctor came to tell her that the boy had Down's Syndrome, she was not at all upset. She says matter-of-factly, "I was on cloud nine at the thought of receiving the blessing of a special child!" Although she quickly admits: "I have never found any other parent with such a positive reaction to news that their baby was not 'normal.'" When Arnold was 14, Judith had an experience that seemed to explain her overwhelming joy at being entrusted with a handicapped child.

In the midst of a past-life regression, Judith found herself in a rural setting in the French Alps. She was married to a peasant farmer, and the couple had goats and made cheese, which Judith took into the market. During the scene, Judith realized that her breasts were gorged and that she was in terrible grief. She came to understand that she had given birth to a handicapped child and her husband had taken the infant away to a convent where the child might be taken care of. Judith recalls: "Although he did it because I would not have the time to be able to care for such a baby and still do all of the tasks that were necessary for our survival, I was still very angry." Her husband was stern and domineering, and during the reverie Judith saw that she had grown old and died as a very bitter and lonely woman.

The meaning of the experience became clear as Judith understood that her domineering husband had reincarnated as her son: "In that life he had given away the handicapped child, in this life he had to face being handicapped himself."

When Arnold was a teenager, Judith began to see some of the domineering and controlling behavior that the boy had exhibited in his previous incarnation; however, since she recognized its source, she was able to help Arnold work through it. She also believes that the way he was raised was extremely helpful in enabling him to work through some of the previous domineering behavior: "I think that a great deal of healing took place. Arnold was raised in a very stable home with lots of love and adoring brothers and sisters. Even now, in his thirties, he is so happy. By his own choice, he lives in a group home and is so happy and blesses so many by his loving spirit."

Today, Judith understands why more than forty years ago she felt such joy when the doctor informed her of Arnold's condition: "I had been pining away for that handicapped child, and the universe finally sent me a child that I could take care of as I had once desired. I was overjoyed."

In another instance, Beverly Stevens, who is now in her sixties, recalls the challenging relationship she once had with her daughter: "Starting when Amy was two years old, she and I could not seem to get along. I loved her but there was a two-way antagonism that troubled me and estranged us through her early adulthood." The animosity between she and Amy continued until Beverly was in her forties and attended a workshop that dealt with the subject of past lives. During the program she experienced a past-life reverie, enabling her to understand the karmic memory between herself and her daughter:

> I clearly saw myself as a young father in New England, circa 1700s. It was winter and I was chopping wood for the fire to warm my large family. I felt strong resentment that my wife was about to give birth to our ninth child, which we could not afford to feed or care for. My only positive thought was the prospect that the child might be a boy—then he could at least help us survive through his own labors.
>
> I was extremely angry when the child was born and I had one more daughter that I didn't want and didn't need. I knew in the midst of the reverie that this daughter had returned as Amy.

Beverly states that the reverie made her feel "humbled and saddened, but very enlightened." Ultimately, the experience became a turning point in healing their relationship. Beverly was able to use it as a means of understanding where the negative feelings had come from as well as consciously deciding to change them. She began working on loving Amy "wholly and without reservation." In time, the negative feelings began to dissipate and Beverly became certain the relationship was finally healed. In fact, when asked how she feels about Amy today, she says without hesitation, "I owe her a lifetime of love."

Additional examples of karmic relationships between children and parents appear in these cases from the Cayce files:

A thirty-three-year-old man became a widower when his pregnant wife gave birth and soon died thereafter of pneumonia. The child was premature and sickly. Suddenly, the man found himself responsible for the care of a young daughter. During the course of his life reading, Cayce explained that in his most recent incarnation he had failed to help a young woman who had come to him in need of his aid. That young woman had returned to him in the present as his daughter. Cayce's advice was simple: "In the experience before this you could have helped and didn't. You better help in the present." (3581-1)

A young woman learned that her controlling father had been her husband in their most recent life together. During that experience, she had forsaken her husband and run off with another man, explaining the rationale behind her father's present-day need to exert control. Complicating the karmic situation, however, in the present, the other man had returned as her boss—twenty-three years her senior, and already married. The two began an affair and despite advice from Edgar Cayce and the frustration of her father and other members of the family, the woman and her boss ran off together, repeating the very same roles they had followed in their most recent incarnation. (2960-1)

A thirty-year-old divorced woman was told that the closeness she felt to her mother was due to the fact that in her most recent incarnation she had been a man and married to the woman who was now her mother. It was this same lifetime that frequently prompted the mother to seek her daughter's advice, rather than the reverse. Apparently, as a man her daughter had often provided groups and individuals with wise counsel, and the mother continued to seek what had once been so readily available. (897-1)

When a fifty-three-year-old woman asked about the past-life connections with her daughter, Cayce explained that there had been several. On one occasion, her daughter had been her mother and in another lifetime her daughter had been a close friend and companion. It was these two experiences that created their relationship dynamic, which the reading described as follows: "Hence at times ye find the daughter as a companion and at times she wants to tell you what to do!" (3615-1)

It is important to point out that the Edgar Cayce material presents the idea that adopted individuals possess the very same karmic connections within their adopted families as do children who are raised by their birth parents. In fact, the readings suggest that spiritual laws work to bring individuals into the very relationships needed at a soul level. Those spiritual laws maneuver situations in the material world so that those children end up in specific homes, regardless of whether or not adoption has been involved. As a case in point, one woman was told that her son had not come by accident or happenstance, but as a means of helping him learn a lesson he needed as a soul: "For this association has not been by chance, but that ye may be in thine own life ever that upon which [your son] may rely for all that is holy, all that is beautiful, all that represents what home really means." (2272-1)

When a professor asked about the past-life connection with his adopted son, Cayce stated that the two had often been together. Three of the most notable previous incarnations included a lifetime when the French military forces had aided the American colonies in their battle for independence. At that time father and son had been members of the French troops—the father serving as a commander over his present-day son. Previous to that experience, the two had been together during a life in Palestine in which the son had served as his father's religious instructor. In one of their earliest incarnations, the two had apparently been married in Atlantis (2246-1).

The foster woman of a twelve-year-old boy inquiring about the past-life connection with the youth was told that she was simply continuing the relationship she had once had with the boy when he had been her own son (603-1). A forty-nine-year-old woman was told that she had essentially adopted her adopted son before, during an experience at the time of Jesus (2787-1).

The adoptive parents of a three-year-old boy and a tenth-month-old boy were informed that both children had been with them previously, as well as with one another. The three-year-old had served in the capacity of sort of governor in Egypt when his younger brother had been an interpreter of the law. At the time the two boys had been close friends. In Persia they had also been together, when the elder boy had served as an emissary. The reading stated that the two boys had purposefully chosen to be brothers in this life in order to learn from one another. (3340-1 and 3346-1).

A contemporary example of adoption in which the attempted soul lessons did not appear to turn out quite so well is told in the story of Heidi and Ben Foster, a couple who were unable to conceive children, so they adopted a daughter and named her Janice. Heidi never kept the adoption a secret from her daughter. Instead, since she believed in karma and reincarnation she simply told Janice that their coming together as a family had been prearranged from the very beginning. Although Ben never took to having a daughter the way Heidi did, one day Janice surprised her mother with the statement: "One time daddy was a man and he shot me and you were the doctor." Although Heidi asked for additional information, her daughter simply looked at her dubiously, as if to say, "Surely you remember!"

According to Heidi, Janice and her adopted father were never close. When Heidi sought a divorce from Ben when her daughter was only nine, it appeared to have little effect on the girl. A few years later when Janice was a teenager, she told her mother: "I'm glad you divorced him. He would have never let me do what I need to do with my life."

Ben remarried and moved out of state with his new wife and stepchildren. He made little attempt to communicate with Janice, and when she spent over two years in Japan for school he never even wrote one letter.

A few years passed and, when Janice was 25, Ben died unexpectedly. Shortly thereafter Janice had a dream in which she was driving her car with the sunroof open and looked up to see Ben trying to get her attention. She told him to go away and closed the sunroof.

Heidi is certain that her daughter and ex-husband came together to heal their karmic memory from the past. She is just as certain that their connection with one another is far from over. According to Heidi, "I have concluded that the two of them definitely have some negative karma, and that it was not resolved in this life." Obviously the two will have to try to meet it at some point in the future.

Katie Eubanks states that "there was a time when I felt overwhelmed in dealing with Dawn," one of her adopted daughters. Dawn had anorexia and the toll on her daughter as well as on the entire family was often more than Katie could handle. Dawn was their first and Katie and her husband subsequently had three additional children. In addition to four children, Katie's role as a schoolteacher entailed the many demands of students on a daily basis. Katie admits, "There were many occasions when my students left me frazzled and my own children completely consumed me."

Without discussing her personal situation, one day Katie obtained a psychic reading from a visiting intuitive. During the reading, the psychic described a past life when Katie had experienced a series of miscarriages, each time "sighing a sigh of relief that there was not the bearing of a child." Obviously, she did not want the responsibility of having children of her own. Eventually, however, she did have a child, a son. Unfortunately, she abandoned her son to others while the boy was still relatively young.

Katie suddenly realized that Dawn had been the child she had once abandoned: "We had sought her out and adopted her as a tiny baby. She was vital in our lives—without her, I'm certain we would not have had any other children. Katie also understood that the many demands of children placed upon her was a karmic balance to having once neglected her responsibilities. That understanding proved extremely helpful, facilitating a new awareness and an approach that helped Katie get through even the most difficult of times.

Eventually, Dawn received the treatment she needed for anorexia and is today a grown woman with a family of her own. As for Katie, she cannot imagine her life without children: " I am reaping the fruits of my new understanding. I experience so much joy and love from my marriage, my children and my grandchildren, and even from my students. My life feels fulfilled."

An example of attempting to work through a negative parent–child memory from the past is contained in the story of Ruth Peterson and Ellen Norris. Both women were in their thirties when they meet one another through Ellen's occupations as a manicurist and a cashier. They became friendly acquaintances.

Ruth was a longtime enthusiast of the Edgar Cayce material and after she had known Ellen long enough to feel comfortable mentioning the subject, she volunteered Cayce's name as an individual who might be of assistance, as Ellen suffered with polio. Ruth had had a number of her own readings, including life, relationship and health readings. In fact, Edgar Cayce told Ruth that in her most recent past life she had been a saloon entertainer in the Old West at the same time that Cayce had been a drifter and a "ne'er do well," and the two had become friends. It was in that same incarnation that Ruth had apparently abandoned a daughter into the care of Indians.

Ellen followed Ruth's advice and obtained both health and life readings. Through the information she learned that the polio was the karmic result of her inflicting bodily harm upon others in a previous incarnation. What came as a greater surprise, however, was that the reading suggested that Ellen had been the very daughter that Ruth had abandoned in the Old West. Cayce went on to say that Ruth's karmic memory of having abandoned a child could be healed in the present by helping Ellen with her polio:

> We find that the entity was a child of . . . [Ruth Peterson] . . . we find that here, in the present experience, much of that as karmic forces in *that* sojourn by that mother, may be met in the present by her ministry to this entity.
>
> Then, keep thou the faith. And indeed may that mother [Ruth] find herself in that love, in that *needed* activity in self, to be—herself—consistent; that there may be brought those helps not only to the body here, but the fullness of the purpose towards creative influences in the life.   2778-2

In order to treat the condition, Cayce recommended ongoing massage as well as the use of a heat cabinet and electrical stimulation to various parts of the body. Because she had such faith in the Cayce information, Ruth Peterson undertook the task of providing the treatments.

Within six months, Ellen's condition had improved dramatically; however, something that Ruth had not foreseen began to take place in that Ellen appeared to relish the role of patient. Ruth Peterson eventually made a report in the 1950s to the Edgar Cayce Foundation, describing what had transpired:

> . . . because I felt so sorry to see anyone in such a physical condition, I made arrangements for Miss [Norris] to have a room (and board) with my mother, who lived right across the street from me, and further engaged my father to make a rubdown table—had the heat cabinet made and wired, and generally setting everything in order so that the treatments could be carried out . . . In the final analysis, I did all of the massaging. So far as I can remember now, the treatments extended for almost 2 years, beginning in August 1942, and running until May, 1944.
>
> During the course of treatments, I learned that the patient had been in and out of hospitals or institutions for Polio from the time she was stricken until her late 'teens. At least 3 or 4 major operations were performed on her feet and legs and thighs, to relieve the drawing in her legs as well as prevent the toe, ankle and knee joints from becoming crystallized. She wore braces which fitted around the thighs, holding the weight of her body from her hips up, when she walked. She spoke often of having no home life and felt that she was not wanted by her parents and in particular—that her mother didn't wish to care for her. I have no way of knowing whether or not this was true, but she felt her "rejection" strongly, and often referred to it.
>
> Three months after starting the treatments the patient was able to stand without crutches or braces, and for the first time in her life bore her weight on her legs. However, she could not keep her balance, not stand for any length of time.
>
> By the spring of 1943 the improvement was so marked that the muscles were beginning to respond; for instance her toes,

and the muscles inside the knee would move. The feet and toes which hung from the ankle as if they were broken, showed signs of control, with the texture of the skin changing. Thus, in the first months, her progress was outstanding and her attitude was optimistic, construction, and expectant . . .

By January, 1943, she was beginning to look forward to the attention the treatments were providing her with. The focus of purpose apparently shifted from getting well to *retaining the care*. As she persisted in this attitude, the therapy sessions became strained, and disturbing to both of us. The insistence on personal attentions—perhaps seeking the "babying" she had felt deprived of all her life, made it necessary that we attempt to reach an understanding of what our individual purposes and desires were. At this point I asked her, "Would your rather have the personal attention, or would you rather walk?" and she replied, "I'd rather have your personal attention, if I would have to choose between the two."   2778-6 Report File

When the relationship became strained, a second life reading was obtained in which Cayce clarified the responsibility each bore toward the other. Although Ruth had abandoned her daughter, the karmic experience of polio was not Ruth's responsibility. In addition, the readings stated that Ruth abandonment had not been "premeditated," but "rather as of stress of circumstance."

When Ellen threatened repeatedly to quit her treatments, Ruth talked her out of it. This went on for some time until the day came when Ellen refused to have any further treatments. According to Ruth's report: "She said to me one day, 'I'm not going to take any more treatments,' and this time I made no effort to talk her out of it. She left Virginia Beach and I did not see her again."

Occasional communication did continue between the two and it was learned that Ellen had improved enough to discard the leg braces and was able to use short crutches, "almost like canes . . . much better and less confining than the old ones." Ellen also kept up correspondence with greeting, birthday, and Christmas cards to Ruth and several members of Ruth's family. The last notations in Ellen's file suggest that multiple times throughout the 1970s she requested additional information from A.R.E., as well as various copies of her readings.

A contemporary example of past-life abandonment is told by a mother who says, "It was extremely difficult raising a child who constantly seemed to resent me. I spent years questioning what I had done to be so hated by my daughter." It was only after the girl married and had a child of her own that mother and daughter began a constructive relationship with one another: "after my granddaughter was born, our relationship had a complete turnaround."

It was several years later during a reverie at a conference program dealing with the subject of past lives that the woman finally got a possible glimpse of the karmic problem. The past-life reverie also gave her an understanding of the feet and leg pain that had been a problem for much of her life.

During the reverie, the woman saw herself as a Jewish woman in the Holy Land who had fallen in love with a Christian Knight who had come to fight the Crusades. Their love eventually led to a pregnancy and the woman gave birth to daughter, whom she left behind to follow her knight after he returned home. During the reverie she saw herself walking hundreds of miles and perishing before she found him. Her abandoned infant had returned as her present-day daughter, and the resentment the girl possessed finally had a rationale explanation. The awareness of their past connection was the impetus that finally enabled the woman to begin healing their relationship.

The Edgar Cayce readings frequently related histories in which parents and children are brought together in a relationship to learn from one another. Sometimes that learning is challenging and difficult, on other occasions that learning is facilitated by example and through love. This process of personal growth and development is simply the means by which each individual meets his or her karmic memory—the means by which each individual meets self. As Cayce told the parents of an eleven-year-old boy:

Yet oft, as we find here, individuals again and again are drawn

together that there may be the meeting in the experience of
each that which will make them aware of wherein they, as
individuals (individual entity and soul), have erred respecting experiences in materiality or soul life even. For the soul
lives on   . . . 693-11

From the Edgar Cayce readings as well as contemporary examples it
is clear that family relationships are much more complex than may be
observed at face value: They involve an ongoing process of karmic
experiences and memories from the past playing out against the dynamics of free will in present time.

4

Karmic Relationships Between Siblings

Then the entity became associated with many of those that are in the entity's own household in the present, and their contacts, their aids, their fallings away, are necessary for the developments of all so associated in the present.   378-12

&

The Edgar Cayce's readings indicate that every individual within a family generally has strong karmic ties with every other member of his or her family. Simply stated, a family's interconnectedness with each other is essentially a complex archaeological dig of past lives and historical experiences that cannot help but influence present–day interactions. To be sure, the strong subconscious memories that each individual possesses of every other family member can lead to intense disagreements, anger and frustration, but it may just as likely contribute to lasting friendships, joy, and some of the deepest connections individuals experience.

In regards to the workings of family karma and the best response to that karmic memory, the Edgar Cayce material suggests that there are essentially two things to keep in mind: (1) Relationships pick up exactly where they have been left off; in other words, there is often a continuity of expression (negatively or positively) in every relationship; and, (2)

Regardless of past-life memories that are influencing a present-day relationship, free will remains the strongest determinant of how that relationship will evolve.

The Edgar Cayce information often reminded individuals of the importance of free will and encouraged them to keep their focus on the
here and now. For example, when a thirty-six-year-old woman asked
for further clarification about a past-life experience when she had apparently had problems with her sister, Cayce encouraged her to keep
her focus on the present: " . . . know—as just indicated—you are having
the same problems with the same individuals in the present." (288-48)

In regards to the lawful continuity of relationships picking up exactly where they left off, Cayce told a brother and sister that their challenges were simply the same issues from the past that hadn't been
"worked out." The problem had manifested in the present when the
brother gave bad financial advice about a business dealing to his sister.
In the course of the reading, Cayce assured the sister that the problem
could be "righted," enabling them to have a positive relationship with
one another and correcting what had once gone wrong. (1000-14)

On another occasion, a twenty-one-year-old law student was told
that he and his younger brother had come into the same family, "choosing the same mother" in the process because of their closeness in a past
life in Palestine. At that time the student had been in some position of
authority and his younger brother had served in the capacity of counselor. Cayce stated that although they had often disagreed during that
experience (and would inevitably do so in the present), it had not affected the close bond between them. (2542-1 and 2677-1)

A twenty-three-year-old woman learned that the ongoing resentment and rivalry she felt from her brother was traceable to their shared
experience in Rome during the formation of the early Church. Apparently at that time in Church history women could hold positions of
spiritual authority, and her brother had become jealous and resentful
when she was elevated to Church deaconess—surpassing his own position of authority in the Church. Cayce suggested that the karmic
memory of that experience was at the heart of his resentment (2803-2).

Being more positive in nature, two sisters learned that their present-day reliance upon one another was simply the continuation of the same type of relationship they had once shared in ancient Egypt, when the two had been close friends and often counseled with and depended upon one another (958-3).

An interesting case history of sibling karma is found in the story of Anna Campbell and her sister, Vera. For as long as she could remember, the sisters had disliked one another. From Anna's perspective it always seemed as though Vera had been competing with her—at home, at school, and among their friends. Although Vera was the eldest, she had come across as being extremely jealous; she didn't want Anna to share her friends, her toys, or even her secrets. The conflict between them had been so routine that their mother eventually gave up all hope of ever reconciling the two. In fact, she once told them, "You'll have to fight it out between the two of you." And fight it out they did.

Of six children in the Campbell household, they were the only two that always had a problem with one another. To make matters worse, as the only girls they had been forced to share a room. At one point the anger between them had caused one of the sisters to take a piece of chalk and draw a line across the wooden floor. And, according to Anna, from that time forward: "Vera had her side of the room, and I had mine." While they were growing up, frequently each had pretended that the other did not even exist.

As time passed and the two grew to adulthood, problems persisted between them. Anna once admitted to Cayce biographer Gina Cerminara that Vera was "so secretive that she didn't even want me to know how many pairs of hose she owned," and that Vera seemed to feel justified in taking anything that belonged to her sister: "She always felt quite free to take anything that was mine—first without my knowing it and eventually it didn't matter whether I knew it or not." (1523-11 Report File). Eventually Anna married and the relationship with her sister deteriorated to the point that Vera couldn't even stand to be in the same room as the couple.

Because of a health condition, Anna eventually came to Edgar Cayce for a reading. The effectiveness of his physical recommendations prompted her to seek out additional information in numerous readings

about her health, her past lives, her marriage, and a variety of relationships. In fact, it was during one of her follow-up readings that Anna
asked for information about the karmic connection with her sister in
the following question: "What has been the past association with my
sister, Vera, that has brought about the apparent antagonistic attitude
toward one another? Just how should I meet this situation for our mutual development?" (1523-11)

Cayce replied that in their most recent incarnation the two had
known each other in the Tidewater, Virginia, area. At the time, Vera had
been married to a man who had become quite ill. Rather than attending to the needs of her husband, Vera kept herself busy with other
duties and obligations, apparently allowing her husband to fend for
himself. However, another woman in town took pity on the man and
nursed him back to health. The other woman had been Anna and the
man had been none other than Anna's present-day husband. During
that experience, Vera became resentful and bitter because in her mind
another woman had stolen the affections of her husband. At the same
time, Anna resented Vera for essentially abandoning her husband. Cayce
described the situation, as follows:

> In that experience we find that in the Tidewater area they were
> antagonists for the companionship of the present husband. Not
> that the entity took the husband away from the sister, but be-
> cause of their associations, because of their companionship,
> because of the willingness to bring encouragement and to
> nurse the entity back to life, there came first that of jealousy,
> then suspicion and then hate.
>
> Thus, as indicated in the present experience of each, they
> are each suspicious of the other—more than hating or misjudg-
> ing the other.   1523-11

In terms of how they could heal their relationship in the present, the
reading encouraged Anna to give her sister hope, help, confidence, love,
harmony and peace. Because of their family connection as well as the
fact that they lived in close proximity to one another, the reading also

suggested that the two would have frequent "association and companionship." Cayce encouraged Anna with the following: "Sow seeds of confidence, even though they are trampled upon. But don't sow them and expect them to be trampled upon! Be hurt whenever they are, yes—but do it again and again!"

Although the advice was not easy, over the years Anna continued to work on her relationship with Vera. When the parents of the two sisters grew old and became ill and the sisters had to help take care of them, the situation provided more than a decade of opportunities to continue to work with their feelings toward one another. Eventually, Anna even admitted that the two could now "tolerate" one another. However, just being tolerant would not finish their work together.

Late in life Anna and Vera found themselves thrown together as each other's closest relative. When she was nearly eighty, Vera became bedridden with no one to care for her except for her seventy-year-old sister. The situation lasted for two years, and although Anna had nursing assistance in caring for her sister, in a very real sense they had many opportunities to be alone together and talk, and reminisce, and think of days gone by. Toward the end of Vera's life it seemed as though all animosity that had existed between them was finally gone. In fact, two days before she died, with words carrying a great deal of emotion and sincerity Vera whispered to Anna, "I hope we can be sisters again."

Since relationship roles frequently change throughout a soul's various incarnations, the Edgar Cayce readings often present case histories in which one-time brothers and sisters returned in different roles, or examples in which previous past-life relationships resulted in a brother-sister experience in the present. The following two contemporary case histories tell stories in which past-life siblings returned to pick up their close relationships, but assumed different roles in the present.

In the first example, a man in his twenties became good friends with a woman in her thirties through their mutual interest in a spiritual organization. Their relationship began when on numerous occasions the two had found themselves at the same conference or social function and were drawn together. Rather than being a romantic connection, their friendship seemed more like that of a brother and sister; in fact,

the man even began calling the woman, "Sis." At one particular conference in which the two were in attendance the source of their friendship
became clear during a past-life reverie. In the reverie, the woman saw a
past life when she was a member of an Indian tribe out west and extremely close to one of the warriors, who was her brother. In the midst
of the reverie, she suddenly realized that her brother from the past had
returned as her present-day friend. Perhaps, surprisingly, during the very
same reverie, the man had simply been thinking about his female friend
and wondering, "I wonder if I knew her before?" All at once he heard a
loud voice register inside his head: "SHE WAS YOUR SISTER!" After the
reverie, the two shared the synchronistic experience with one another.

The second example is the story of Allen Brockman who had been
living with his girlfriend for a couple of years but could not bring himself to ask her to marry. According to Allen, "I could never understand
why I loved her and cared about her, but I was not 'in love' with her."

Because Allen had long worked with his dreams—often asking a
question before falling asleep and getting an answer in his dreams—he
decided to ask about his relationship. That night he saw his girlfriend
living in Scotland during a previous period in history. In the same
dream he saw himself as a female, and it became clear from the dream
that he and his girlfriend had once been sisters.

When Allen awoke he understood their present-day connection. He
also understood why the love he felt was not the same kind of love he
had hoped to find in a marriage relationship. Shortly thereafter, the two
amicably agreed to break up as boyfriend and girlfriend.

Another contemporary example of karma between siblings in which
the feelings in the relationship were not completely amicable is the
story of a middle-aged man who describes his relationship with his
sister as follows: "We have always had strong feelings for each other, but
at the same time I would say that our relationship is quite distant."
When the two are together at family functions and holiday get-
togethers, there is a strong recognition of an emotional bond—a bond
that is just as likely to prompt frustration and animosity as it is love and
understanding. Part of their present-day relationship dynamic is that in
between family functions there is no attempt by either brother or sister

to maintain contact. The basis of their sibling karma finally seemed to have a rational explanation when the brother caught a glimpse of their most recent lifetime together:

> I saw a scene in which she was my wife during the colonial period. We lived in Boston where I was a doctor. We had a daughter that had become ill, and in spite of my medical training, I was unable to save her, and she died. The tragedy devastated our marriage. My wife withdrew from me, as I withdrew from her, and our marriage deteriorated. In the midst of this experience, I "knew" that this situation was at the heart of our present relationship dynamic.

A story that details how karmic memory can surface in everyday life is told by Wanda Groves. Now in her fifties, Wanda recalls as a child how she used to dream about a little dark-haired girl. The dreams lasted well into high school and Wanda assumed they were simply a vision of a child that would be hers one day in the future. She now knows that the dreams were past-life in nature and that she was actually glimpsing a past-life version of herself:

> I eventually came to understand that the girl was about nine years old and lived around the late 1890s. She came from a very close-knit family and was particularly close to an older brother. She died before her 10th birthday of complications from a cold and pneumonia.

What made the recall information so interesting to Wanda was the fact that her present life seemed to mirror a major invent from the previous lifetime; when she was nine years old she was hospitalized with pneumonia and nearly died: "At the time, I was terrified that I was going to die." She survived and has been health conscious ever since, "taking care of myself through good nutrition, exercise and check-ups." In terms of the family karma from that experience, Wanda says with certainty, "I now know that my older son, with whom I am very close, had been my brother back when I died of pneumonia."

Another example of karma between siblings from the Cayce files is the story of Anthony and John Williams—two brothers who each had physical readings from Edgar Cayce. John was forty-one-years old and two years older than Anthony when he sent a letter to Cayce asking for additional information about his relationship with his brother: "I wonder whether you would be kind enough, to give me another reading which would throw light on the relationship between my brother Anthony and myself and also give me some rules for my own conduct in this relationship." (2564-3 Report File) According to notations eventually made in John's file, the relationship was marked with jealousy and frequent problems in spite of the fact that John felt that he had always tried to help Anthony, who suffered with multiple sclerosis.

The reading highlighted three incarnations in early America, Rome and ancient Egypt. Cayce stated that the basis of their problematic relationship was essentially because of a difference in motivating ideals in those lifetimes. In John's case, the reading stated that he was generally motivated by freedom of the individual, including freedom of worship as well as the freedom to work together for a collective idea (such as the establishment of the United States). Conversely, Anthony's approach had generally been more controlling and fear-based, even going so far as to advocate government by intimidation. According to the reading, "These different attitudes that arise are as the basis of the disturbances that are the experience of each in the present." (2524-4) In terms of healing their relationship in the present, Cayce gave John the following advice:

> And in thy dealings with thy brother, meet rather that as would be if conditions were reversed; being patient, being understanding; not as preachments but rather as following of precepts and living the ideal that is manifest in the word of the entity.
>
> And let thy prayer ever be, in this direction:
>
> *Father, God! Speak thou to me in words that I may understand. But let me, O God, speak ever to my brother in deeds, rather than words.*
>
> These (words), in the state of each, only cause disputations. Yet these conditions may be met, if there is the manifesting

of patience and brotherly love.   2524-4

As previously mentioned, individuals in adopted families have the same kind of karmic connections from the past as those in birth families. For example, parents of two adopted boys wanted to know if they had ever been related "by blood or marriage" to their sons. They were told that they had all been together as a family in Ancient Persia, where one of the boys had been essentially a governor. That same son had talents in politics and was very self-certain, whereas his younger brother was much more shy. The reading said that, in part, the two boys had chosen to come back again into the same family by way of adoption so that the younger boy could learn how to feel positive about himself from his elder brother. Previously the two had also share a strong social connection in Egypt at a time when "much was brought to light" in terms of spiritual truths and the physical, mental and spiritual development of humankind. (3346-1 and 3340-1)

Another example is that of a boy and a girl who had been adopted into the same family at different times. The two frequently fought with one another, causing their adopted mother to ask about their past-life connection. Cayce explained that in various periods in history they had been members of opposing groups, including in Rome and in Egypt. In the present, the adopted parents were encouraged to "temper" the children's responses to one another, provide them each with a spiritual foundation and instill hope and purposefulness into their upbringing. In this manner, their present-day relationship problems could be healed. (2690-1 and 2691-1)

The following cases from the Cayce readings offer more examples of sibling karma:

A woman found herself widowed at a very young age and, having nowhere else to turn, she moved in with her brother. For years, the two lived together as housemates, apparently becoming very close because of the arrangement. Cayce stated that part of the karmic memory that had drawn the two together was the fact that they had been together in ancient Egypt. During that experience they had aggressively disagreed and opposed one another in regards to a rebellion that was taking place against the king. Although they eventually worked through some of the issues in that experience, their present relationship had finally enabled them to heal whatever negative karmic memory had remained. (3564-2 and 3062-2)

When parents of a five-year-old girl and a baby boy obtained a reading for their daughter and asked why the girl had chosen to be born into her present family, the reply suggested that her entrance would ultimately enable each member of the family to learn something about themselves. In the language of the readings: "or the meeting of much in each." (1635-3)

On another occasion, a forty-one-year-old cook asked Edgar Cayce why she had always felt distant from her brother and sisters. Cayce explained that during a past life in England during the uprising against Charles II, she had tried to be an influence for political calm and diplomacy. However, members of her community were not pleased with her endeavors and managed to have her evicted from her home and sent to France. According to the readings, the individuals responsible for her banishment had incarnated as her present-day siblings. (2624-1)

A forty-seven-year-old woman was told that during the early formation of the Church in Laodicea, she had been married to the disciple who oversaw that group of the Church's faithful. When she asked how she had been related to her mother and father at the time, Cayce replied that they had been, "A brother and a sister, in that particular experience." (1468-3)

A forty-three-year-old woman asked for additional insights into her past-life connections with members of her family. Cayce replied that some of the roles were similar and that some had reversed (such as parent and child), but that regardless of the specific relationship there were "needs" in the present that had come as a karmic response or an outgrowth to that previously experienced. The overall purposefulness of these relationships—approached aright—was for the development and growth of everyone involved:

> And these become then the real reasons—if there is as a reason—rather because the brother was then the sister, or the sis-

ter rather then as the relationships of the companion . . . [but] in the present the relationships are such that if the relationships are related to Creative Forces, as they are expressed in the fruits of the spirit, and these exercised in the relationships, the development of body, mind and soul becomes in its proper relationship in the present.   338-4

On another occasion, quibbling siblings from an incarnation in the early settling of Canada had returned in the present to work through their frequent dissension over minor things, only this time their relationship was that of husband and wife. Cayce told the couple that the same attitude they often possessed as brother and sister often crept into their present activities; however, they had gradually become more amicable in working together than they had previously. In fact, Cayce told the woman: "Ye are working it out beautifully! Keep it in the same way and manner—to give and forgive, counsel and re-counsel, one with the other." (2174-1)

When a twenty-seven-year-old woman inquired about the advisability of moving out of her family's apartment and finding a place of her own because of the difficulties she was having with family members, Cayce responded that if she was able to do it, it would actually be best to try to work things out before moving. Knowing that the situation was difficult, Cayce provided a couple of ways of looking at the situation. He said that if she was unable to be other than antagonistic toward her family members, or they could only be antagonistic towards her, then it would be better to move. If she moved immediately, however, she needed to know that it would lead to spite and animosity, and additional karma in the future. The best approach would be for her to discover how she could be helpful and assist them in the present:

But if there is sought by the entity for not the differences that exist in the minds of the family and the associations but as to how the entity may be a help to those in the family in finding their relationships to Creative Forces, this will make for the better surroundings, making the security of the entity in its

> abilities for stabilizing itself in a much surer and a much bet-
> ter means or manner.   1436-3

Along the same lines, when a thirty-nine-year-old photographer asked, "What do you suggest would be best for me to do regarding my family relations?" The reading reminded him that he was meeting his own self. He was encouraged to meet all of his family obligations and to keep the following approach in mind: "As ye would have them do to you, do ye even so to them." (876-1)

On one occasion, when a thirty-five-year-old accountant whose sister had already obtained a reading asked the following question: "Do I owe the members of my family anything and what?" Cayce responded:

> There is a duty, an obligation that ye owe *self* in the relation-
> ship to *every* member of the family; as *every* member owes same
> to thee; to make the associations constructive and each better
> for having been thrown or drawn together.
>
> For nothing happens as by accident, but that the glory of
> the Father may be manifested in the doings and the relation-
> ships of each individual as one to another.   1432-1

Families are drawn together as a means of enabling every individual to become a better person for having been with other family members. There is also a lawfulness as to why certain individuals are drawn into a family at a given time. As one reading puts it, "No association or experience is by chance, but is the outgrowth of a law—spiritual, mental or material." (2753-2) Therefore, every individual is drawn into his or her family as a means of learning specific lessons pertinent to that individual's soul growth and development. Whether or not those lessons are learned at any given time remains a matter of free will; however, the readings suggest that eventually each of those lessons will be learned—it is simply a matter of time. As Cayce told one woman: "Know that this has not been completed in the present, and thus is to be *met in each!* Then why not now?" (1523-6)

5

Miscellaneous Karmic Relationships

> Yet oft, as we find here, individuals again and again are drawn together that there may be the meeting in the experience of each that which will make them aware of wherein they, as individuals (individual entity and soul), have erred respecting experiences in materiality or soul life even. For the soul lives on . . .   693-3

An underlying premise in the Edgar Cayce readings is that individuals who have a strong emotional feeling toward one another—positively or negatively—generally have karmic memory that constantly influences their present relationship. In other words, oftentimes people respond to one another with greater depth of emotion than might seem appropriate to an objective observer because those individuals are not only responding to an incident in the present but, in all likelihood, to other experiences that have ever occurred between them throughout all time and space. In spite of these past–life memories and the subsequent influences they have, however, Cayce was adamant in maintaining that free will remained the strongest influence in any given relationship because, although there may be negative patterns and inclinations that exist at an unconscious level, those "impulses" do not need to be reenergized or given power in the present.

The importance of free will was emphasized in a reading, for a woman in her forties who was a strong supporter of Edgar Cayce and his work. She was extremely close to her nieces and nephews, for whom she obtained readings. One of her nephews was thirteen at the time of his reading and the aunt and nephew apparently wavered between a very amicable relationship and one in which each seemed to be a source of irritation to the other. When the question was asked in the boy's reading as to whether they would be closely associated throughout his life or end up separating, Cayce responded that the answer was not set; instead it had to do with the use of their will in the present: "This depends to be sure upon the activities . . . No life, no individual is set! It is not a line; it deviates. For the will of each may change the relationships." (1235-1)

Cayce went on to explain that the greatest source of their connection was the karmic memory from a lifetime in Rome in which the two had been friends. During that experience, the nephew had often provided guidance that his present-day aunt depended upon. In the present, their roles had been reversed and the aunt now found herself in the role of guiding the youth, especially in terms of his spiritual direction. Apparently, the conflict existed because not only did the nephew now find himself in a subservient position but at a subconscious level the aunt realized that she could no longer turn to her former friend for help, as she had done in the past. When the question was asked as to whether or not the relationship had the potential to be beneficial for the youth in the present, Cayce again turned the answer over to the application of individual will: "Depends upon the application again. *Everything* in the experience depends upon the application. How wilt thou use thy opportunities? if for weal or for woe? These are *not* set!"

The readings also repeat that there is an underlying purposefulness behind every relationship and experience encountered by a soul. For example, during the course of a reading given to a thirty-five-year-old musician interested in past lives, work prospects and his personal relationships, Cayce stated that wherever an individual found himself or herself in the present is an opportunity to be a meaningful experience:

Yet, let the entity know that it is not by chance that it has

entered this experience at this time, but the life is a purposeful experience; and the place in which it finds itself in the
present is that from which it may use the present abilities, the
present faults, the present failures—yea, the present virtues—
in fulfilling that purpose for which the soul manifests in the
material or three-dimensional plane.   2421-2

On another occasion, a forty-one-year-old woman interested in the
karmic connection between herself and her daughter was told: "It is
true for the entity, and for most individual souls manifesting in the
earth, that nothing, no meeting comes by chance. These are a design or
a pattern. These patterns, however, are laid out by the individual entity.
For there are laws." (2620-2)

Edgar Cayce frequently emphasized the lawfulness of karma by para-
phrasing a line from the New Testament: " . . . for whatsoever a man
soweth, that shall he also reap." (Galatians 6:7) For example, when a
fifty-six-year-old woman had questions about the karmic relationships
between herself and various family members, she was told: "Learn the
law; that ye reap what ye sow! The manner in which ye measure to
others, it will be measured to thee again! That is an unchangeable law!
Then, live the law; be the law, as respecting such." (2185-1)

Along the same lines, a thirty-eight year-old member of the U.S Trea-
sury Department's Secret Service was reminded:

   . . . each soul meets that it—the soul—has builded in the experiences.
   For the law of the universe, the law of a merciful Father,
   remaineth ever. Though there may be turmoils within the
   earth, though there may be confusions in the elements about
   the earth, the law remains that what ye sow ye reap, what ye
   sow ye must meet.   1205-1

A fifty-six-year-old investment counselor apparently having
problems at work was reminded that his experience was simply a lawful recompense for his own actions in a previous life. In other words,

he was simply meeting himself:

> The entity took advantage of a group. Hence expect a group to take advantage of thee! For what ye measure, it must be, it will be measured to thee. For ye must pay every whit that ye measure to others. And this applies in the future as well as in the past. Do you wonder that your life is in such a mess!
>
> 3063-1

As stated previously, rather than being some type of a punishment or a debt, the karmic memory that enables people to "meet" themselves in their experiences and relationships is ultimately the means through which individuals grow, develop and become more in alignment with their Creator. Oftentimes, that growth entails learning how to love unconditionally—whether it's love of self or love of others. The contemporary story of Hiromi Martin is one such example:

Hiromi admits that for a long time she didn't understand her karmic relationship with her mother–in–law or the lesson that each had been attempting to learn. She was born in Asia, and her own parents immigrated first to Holland and then to the United States. During World War II, her father had spent four years as a POW in a Japanese prison camp. When she became an adult, Hiromi married a United States citizen, a Caucasian. Although close to her husband, she always had a very challenging time with her mother–in–law, who came across as being prejudice about Hiromi's nationality. To make matters worse, because of a series of life events, her mother–in–law lived with her and her husband for over twenty years.

According to Hiromi, her mother–in–law was mean, critical, insulting, and prone to frequent yelling: "For a number of years, I thought I was the cause of the way she treated me, and it was devastating." For years she waited on the woman's every demand: "I felt like an indentured slave whose servitude would never be up." The situation went on for seventeen years, causing Hiromi to become despondent: "I wallowed in feelings of selfishness and despair and I ignored my need to love myself and take care of my health." In the seventeenth year she developed cancer and became convinced that her attitude and hopelessness had depleted her immune system and allowed the cancer to manifest. Hiromi became determined that she would not allow herself to die from the situation.

In addition to following the treatment recommended by her doctor, Hiromi eventually went to a psychic and asked what past-life experience was most affecting her situation in the present. The response was that she had once been an Egyptian slave serving a cruel and arrogant master—eventually she had escaped the situation and was able to live a happy life with a family of her own. It did not take a stretch of the imagination to realize that the master she had once served and despised had returned as her present-day mother-in-law. It is only now that Hiromi realizes the lessons that each had tried to teach the other:

> She tried to teach me the very hard lesson of self-worth and the fact that I didn't need her approval. She needed to learn from me that people of a different color or race are no different than herself—no one is any better or any worse than anyone else. In time, I learned patience and self-worth. I even learned to love myself.

Hiromi did all the right things and she quickly regained her health, and her peace of mind. Within a couple of years, her entire life had changed—her children grew up and left home, she made a new life for herself and no longer felt like the "victim" she had once been. It was only after she had transformed her relationship with her mother-in-law that the elder woman passed on. Rather than dreading their next encounter, Hiromi now thinks of their karmic memory with a different attitude: "I never again want to repeat the history we have had. I no longer have the need to be challenged in order to love myself or to feel my self-worth through another's approval or acceptance. Because I have changed, I hope our next meeting will be one of mutual love and acceptance."

The story of Phyllis Lambert is also one that entails its share of personal challenges. One of the earliest challenges concerned her boyfriend,

Paul, whom she describes as follows:

> Paul was my brother's best friend. He was always a part of our
> family. Paul and I dated through high school and said that we
> would get married. His father was a plumber and he planned
> to follow in his father's footsteps but first he wanted to serve
> his military time. He enlisted in the army. He was killed six
> weeks after his arrival in Vietnam.

Paul's death was devastating but Phyllis got on with her life as best
as she could. She married someone else at eighteen but divorced at
nineteen. She spent two years hitchhiking across the country before
marrying again at twenty–three. She had two sons before getting her
second divorce at twenty–five. She married again at thirty and divorced
three years later. After that, she dated a number of men but avoided any
kind of real commitment. For a long time, it seemed like her life was out
of control: "I was single, working full–time, drinking, raising two sons,
sleeping with anyone who asked, and using recreational drugs (cocaine
and grass)." When her life seemed at its lowest point, Phyllis had a dream
that changed everything:

> It seems that there was a highway. No cars, no trucks, just
> people walking . . . The road was bordered on each side with
> green grass running into the valley . . . I was enjoying the
> walk. Off in the distance the trees were so pretty and so tempt-
> ing that I started to walk in that direction. As I wandered to-
> wards the forest, a man came out. He wore blue jeans, a red
> plaid shirt and tennis shoes. He had dark hair and glasses. As
> we came closer to each other, I realized that this was Paul. But
> Paul was dead—killed years ago in Vietnam!
>
> I was so happy to see him, tears welled into my eyes and
> my heart exploded with happiness. I ran toward him and just
> stared for a minute. He looked just like he always had, only
> older and more mature. He had the same rosy cheeks and the
> same habit of pushing his glasses up his nose with his index

finger. I held him and felt the warmth of his body and smelled the familiar smell that was his alone. I cried from happiness and never questioned why he was there . . .

I wanted so much to stay with Paul, to be in his presence, to talk to him about all of the things that had happened in my life, but he told me I needed to leave. He said that my sons needed me, but he promised that he would be at the end of this road later and we would have forever to talk.

I remember crying, yet feeling so safe and secure and peaceful within myself. It was like getting a breath of clean, cool air after a hot, humid day. Paul told me to hurry and he turned and walked back into the trees. I wanted to follow, but I was torn between him and my boys. But Paul did say that he would be at the end of the road, and I trusted him. I turned and headed back in the direction that I had come.

After she awoke, Phyllis' life was never the same. She is convinced that the dream became a turning point and enabled her to start getting her life in order. She eventually earned an associate's degree in accounting to help her in her career. She focused on raising her sons, and she also became involved in a spiritual discussion group. Eventually, she began having a series of dreams and past-life experiences that convinced her that she had been a "saloon girl" in the 1800s. During a past-life reverie, she got the sense that she had been abandoned by her parents at the age of fifteen in southern Canada and had ended up working in a saloon in Montana as a means of supporting herself. She now realizes that after Paul's death she had picked up a past-life pattern that was connected to her present-day karmic struggles with men:

I understand that each man I've had a relationship with may well be connected to that lifetime in Montana, and other lives as well. I'm aware of a pattern of not trusting men, on insisting that I maintain my "freedom" and independence. I finally understand that some of these patterns don't have to be repeated.

Phyllis is certain that her relationship with Paul was the continuation of a relationship they had shared in the past and will undoubtedly share in the future. The concept of reincarnation has also helped her transform some of her more challenging relationships:

> I know this isn't the end of who I am, and that what I learn and experience will come with me in future lives—it's an ongoing process for us all. I also know that people I deal with today are some of those with whom I've interacted in the past, and will no doubt contend with in the future. This can be comfort as well as a motivation to change a situation today.

In another contemporary example, Lois Holmes describes how past-life recall enabled her to overcome an overeating problem, understand why she had such an affinity to various minorities and realize where her strong connection to her granddaughter came from. Now in her seventies, Lois admits that all of her life she had a problem with her weight and overeating—a problem that is also shared by her granddaughter. Although a Caucasian woman herself, while growing up she often resented white people for their racial prejudice:

> I always felt that I was born into the wrong family. Nobody was like me—they didn't think like me. I loved them, and they loved me but we were so very different in our thinking especially about religion and race. I have always felt a strong connection for the "underdog," no matter who the person was or what color he or she happened to be. I have always felt a strong connection to Native Americans, African Americans, and people from India . . . this was all very different than my upbringing.

After Lois became interested in reincarnation, she had a past–life experience in which she saw herself living in India as a member of the lower class: "I saw myself as a resident of India and I also saw that my present–day granddaughter, with whom I am very close, was my beloved younger sister." During the experience, Lois realized that both she and her younger sister had starved in that lifetime. When it was over, the past-life memory became the impetus she needed to overcome her overeating problem: "I was able to see why I overate in this lifetime. As a result, I have stopped overeating since that recall experience." She was also able to see how being a member of one of India's lower classes enabled her to have an affinity with individuals who were the "underdog" or of a minority. When asked if there was anything she would like to say to family members about her experience, Lois responded:

> I would like to talk to my mother, my dad, my sister, and my brothers—all of who have passed over . . . I would like to tell them all of the things that I have experienced, and how understanding reincarnation has been such a light in my life—answering so many questions. While alive, they would have thought my ideas heresy and even blasphemy. They could not understand why I liked black people or why I was so liberal. I have told my remaining family about my experiences, and at least most of them have seemed pretty open to the ideas I have to share.

A less positive example of karmic memory and being unwilling or unable to work through it is evidenced in the story of two women who were told in their Cayce readings of a strong past-life connection with Edgar Cayce himself. Donna Vincenze was from Virginia Beach, Virginia, and sometimes volunteered to work in Cayce's office; Magdalena Capputto was somewhat of a socialite, who lived in New York City and saw Cayce when he was there on business. Although the two did not know each other personally, both women had been told that they had once had a very close personal relationship with Cayce during the same past life. According to Magdalena's readings, she had been married to Edgar Cayce when he essentially kept what amounted to a Roman mistress; Donna was told that she had been that mistress. One day Magdalene decided to make a trip to Virginia Beach, and Edgar Cayce decided it would make for an interesting experiment to see what would happen when the two women finally met for the very first time. It was Donna who eventually made the following report for the Cayce archives:

> Mr. Cayce told me that Mrs. Capputto was coming to Va. Beach and that he would be most interested in seeing us meet . . . He told me that he had not told her about me—at least he had not identified me, and that when I met her—I would know but she would not. He seemed interested in what her reaction would be to me. It interested me that he did not seem concerned about how I might react to her.
>
> As I recall she arrived on a Monday or Tuesday—of the week—I do not recall what month, but I do remember the weather was very nice. The first time I met her, we picked her up to take her to the Tuesday Night Bible Meeting. Mrs. Cayce, Gladys, Mr. Cayce, Mrs. Capputto and I were the only ones in the car—Actually I do not know what I expected to feel, but I can tell you that I was very surprised to find that I felt very sure of my position—as related to Mr. Cayce and Mrs. Capputto, but the unexpected thing was that I felt very flirtatious. She had planned to stay at the Beach two weeks—but checked out the next day and went back to N.Y. After Mr. Cayce had seen her in N.Y. he told (when he came home) that she explained that she was so upset by my presence that she just had to go home.   1523-16 Report File

A contemporary example of almost reliving karmic memory from the past is told in the story of Alicia Albertson who broke off her three-year relationship with her boyfriend Rick. Alicia admits that even though she initiated the break-up, she was still upset, as she had often contemplated the possibility of marrying Rick. As Alicia recalls, "Even upon our first meeting and all along the way, I just knew that this was an important relationship for us."

Part of the problem had been the fact that Rick seemed to have a "cruel and distant streak" that made life miserable. Even though Alicia

realized that the break–up was for the best, she obtained a reincarnation regression tape by Brian Weiss and tried to get at the heart of her
connection. The regression enabled her to see the karmic memory that
had led to their relationship in the present:

> I very clearly saw myself in 1800s France. I was the wife of a
> very wealthy man, who was older than I. I could see that he
> had dark hair and a beard. He was also very cruel and harsh.
> As a result, I hated my life but I had no way out. I did not have
> the upper hand or any income of my own. I was desperate to
> break away but I didn't know how I could. When I looked
> closely at my husband's face in the reverie, I realized that it
> was Rick.

When the reverie was over, Alicia understood that her three–year
relationship with Rick had been the opportunity to re–script what she
had been unable to change in the past. She also found it interesting that
in this life she had had the "upper hand" all along: she was seven years
older than Rick, she was the one that had been formerly educated, and
her career had been the more financially rewarding.

Peggy McGrath tells an even more positive example of healing a
past–life memory through the use of the will. As background information, Peggy was born in Ireland more than seventy years ago to a Catholic mother and a Protestant father. At the time it was unthinkable that a
Catholic would marry a Protestant, and placing Peggy with her mater-
nal grandmother solved the dilemma of her illegitimate birth. She was
essentially abandoned by her birthparents—her mother was sent off to
England to pursue a nursing career and her father was shipped to India
as part of the British government's police presence. She never met either her mother or father, as her birth had somehow "shamed" them
and they felt forced to completely alter the course of their lives. However, Peggy's grandmother adored her and she had a wonderful upbringing.

Peggy moved to the United States in the 1940s to pursue an education. Eventually, she married and had children of her own. In time, her

children married and had their own children. She was delighted when the time came for her to become a grandmother. Her joy was short-lived, however, when it became apparent that her granddaughter—though only an infant—did not want to be around her: "For whatever reason, she just didn't feel comfortable with me." Because she had always been popular with children, Peggy couldn't understand what the problem was but regardless of how she spoke to, cuddled or held her granddaughter, the baby's attitude did not change. The child did not like her or want to be around her. One night, however, Peggy had a dream that seemed to answer where the problem had originated:

> I was riding a merry-go-round with my favorite aunt, who I knew was deceased, but in the dream she was alive and well. All at once the merry-go-round started going backwards and I realized it was moving back in time. I turned and noticed that my granddaughter was sitting near my aunt and as the merry-go-round continued its journey back in time my granddaughter became my mother. As my mother, she spoke happily with my aunt. My aunt looked at me to make certain I had gotten the message—that this woman who had been forced to change her life because of my birth was now my granddaughter—and when it was clear I understood, my aunt got off at the next stop. I was left alone on the merry-go-round with my mother.

Upon awakening, Peggy knew that she had to heal the relationship with her granddaughter/mother. Immediately, she started praying for their relationship and for their ability to forgive one another. She also worked with meditation. Almost like a silent affirmation, in her mind she began thanking her mother for all of the good things that the woman had been instrumental in bringing to her life. Peggy even thanked her mother for life itself. The approach seemed to work, for gradually, her granddaughter began to change. As Peggy recalls:

> By the time my granddaughter was a toddler, she insisted on coming to visit with me and staying overnight with me. Any

of her tiny problems were brought specifically to me to be solved. As the years passed, anything I ever gave to her became like a special treasure in her eyes, even to this day. When she grew up, I found it especially interesting that she chose her previous career of nursing. This time she took it a step further and became a neo-natal nurse, as though she wanted to make certain that she could help take care of little children, as she had to leave one behind the last time around. She simply adores children.

Peggy states that without the dream, she and her granddaughter might have gone through life ignoring each other, never healing the situation from the past.

Another example of personal healing is evidenced in the past–life story of Nadine Brockman. According to Nadine, it was during a hypnotic regression that she came to the realization that two lifelong personal phobias and her favorite aunt's inability to have children were all connected to the same experience—an experience in which she and her aunt had last been together. Nadine states that throughout her life she has been afraid of two things: having another person touch her head and traveling any distance away from her home:

As far back as I can remember, I hated anyone touching my head or combing my hair. I even refused to go to the beauty shop—preferring instead to cut my own hair. In terms of travel, anytime I had to go somewhere I developed some kind of a sickness: severe dizziness, head colds, middle ear infections, etc.

In part because of her phobias, Nadine eventually went to a regression therapist to see about the possibility of being hypnotized and regressed as a means of being healed of both problems. The results she experienced ended up being instantaneous:

I saw myself as a three-year-old girl, living near the beach in

Sweden. My mother in that lifetime was my childless aunt from the present. One evening I wanted to go out to play but my mother told me it was too late and I needed to go to bed. I was very unhappy with her response, so when she was not looking I saw myself sneak out of the house and run out to the beach to play.

As early evening turned to darkness, I became scared. I was lost. I saw a light atop some rocks so I began climbing what amounted to a cliff. Unfortunately, when I was up quite a ways, I ended up falling off the cliff and smashing my head on the rocks below.

The scene changed and I could see my mother (now aunt) holding me and weeping over me, crying aloud, "I will never have children again."

The experience proved to be very emotional for Nadine. While still in the regression she started crying and saying, "It's all my fault, it's all my fault." The hypnotist reassured her by gently repeating that she had only been a child and had never meant for the tragedy to happen. Still, it really affected her to see her now–aunt in such pain: "I'm closer to her than even my own mother!"

In the end, however, the experience proved to be helpful and heal-ing. Today, it doesn't bother Nadine to have someone else touch her hair and she no longer gets sick when traveling. Not only have the concepts of reincarnation and karma enabled Nadine to make strides in her personal growth and development but she is convinced that they hold the same promise for everyone:

We have the opportunity to stretch and reach our soul's poten-tials. There is a Higher Power, a Source, within each and every one of us. If only people would try to accept life's challenges, to understand that there is a reason for everything. We are solely responsible for creating our reality.

An interesting example of family karma created and played out within the same hundred-year period is told by Angela Anderson. According to Angela, her story began when she was a young girl on a train with her mother traveling from California to Oklahoma. The ride seemed fine until her mother tried to take her from the passenger car to the dining car. Between cars, the noise of the wheels on the tracks was so loud that Angela began to scream and cry until her mother took her back to the passenger car. From that time on Angela had an irrational fear of trains. As she grew older, she noticed other idiosyncrasies developing such as disgust for the sound of the German language and an irrational fear that as a mother she herself would lose a child.

Time passed and eventually Angela married a police officer, became a nurse and had two children: a boy and a girl. Her children were wonderful. Her son liked to draw and seemed especially interested in drawing cars. In addition to her duties as a nurse, she and her husband both taught Baptist Sunday school. For the most part, her life was very good. However, one night she had a terrifying dream:

> I felt during the dream as though I was awake and this was real. I heard the screen door open and looked up into the face of a man standing beside me. The streetlight shone on his face. He was dressed all in black from his feet to his head. Only his face, hair and hands were not covered. His eyes were black and slanted and they had the most evil look I had ever seen. I knew he meant to kill me. I tried to scream and punch my husband but could not make a sound nor could I move a muscle. I was filled with terror. The man stepped toward me and my terror became worse.

Angela forced herself to awaken and was unable to go back to sleep. Still terrified, she was certain that she had seen the face of death. Her husband tried to reassure her that everything was okay, but Angela became convinced that something horrible was about to happen. Her fears proved prophetic one week later when her husband was involved in a car accident with another car while riding with their fifteen-year-old son. Their son was killed instantly and her husband was left a cripple, retaining only the use of one arm. The crash resulted in her husband's onslaught of epilepsy as well as a struggle with severe depression. He also felt guilty for not being able to avoid the accident. Angela herself became very bitter over the loss of their son. For a time it seemed that her husband might not survive his own injuries. At the very least, his work as a police officer was over. Their life as a family was horribly altered and seemed almost impossible to deal with. In addition to all this tragedy, for some reason, Angela had an intense fear of her daughter being raped and often told friends, "I would rather be raped myself than have my daughter raped." The intervention of two people helped to turn Angela's life around. The doctor who saved her husband's life was from India. In addition to helping her husband, the doctor tried to comfort Angela. He encouraged her and told her that in his opinion, "the soul changes bodies like the body changes clothes." His words opened her mind to an entirely new philosophy and according to Angela, "Thus began my current journey toward wisdom and enlightenment." The second individual was a friend and a hypnotherapist who agreed to hypnotize Angela to see if she could discover why this tragedy was a part of her life's experience. To her amazement, while under hypnosis Angela remembered exact details of a past life that seemed to explain the karmic reason behind the tragedy:

> I remembered a life in Poland when I was a Polish Jew named Claude Rainey. I had a jewelry store and a watch repair shop on a corner. My wife was named Edith (I knew she had returned as my daughter in this life) and my son was named Reuben (I knew he had returned as my son). The year was 1943.
>
> In my memory we heard the Nazis coming and all of us went into hiding. I hid behind a showcase inside a wall where money and jewelry were hidden. I could see through a tiny crack in the wall. The Nazis found Reuben and beat, kicked, and stomped him to death. They also found Edith and took turns raping her before they killed her. I did nothing to try and stop them. By the time the Nazis found me, there was

> blood everywhere. Since I was strong, I was sent by train to
> Bergen-Belzen [a Nazi concentration camp]. I knew that my
> husband in this life had been a member of the SS at the camp
> and had been killed during the war. Later I was sent by train
> to Auschwitz, where I was murdered.

The experience explained many things: Angela's fear of trains, her fear of losing a child, her fear about her daughter being raped, her feelings about the German language, even her husband's own injuries seemed to be in recompense for his actions in Nazi Germany.

Since that experience, Angela has come to grips with her son's death. She has even forgiven the man who caused the accident. Because of the events in her life and the people who helped her gain a new understanding, her philosophy has changed to the point where she now believes, "The soul cannot escape itself." She is convinced that her life's experiences have been purposeful, and that the individuals who helped her to change her philosophy were not sent by accident. Twenty years have passed since the accident, and although she still misses her son, she is convinced that he has returned to her family. She is now a grandmother and amazingly her grandson is like her son "in every way." His personality, his appearance and his interaction with family members remind Angela of the son she lost. She adds, "He even draws cars almost identical to those our son used to draw!"

Certainly, past-life experiences influence present-day relationships. As a demonstration of how Cayce's clients experienced this lawful meeting of karmic memory in their own lives, some examples from the files follow:

A sixty-four-year-old woman inquired about her past-life relationship with her son-in-law, an individual whose purposes she often questioned and yet she generally felt very close to him, sometimes even feeling "of one mind." Her reading stated that she had been closely associated with him as a friend on at least two different occasions: in Egypt during the rise of the Hebrew Joseph from prisoner to second-in-command of the country, and also during the second breaking up of the continent of Atlantis. During these experiences the two friends often

found occasion to debate one another. In the present, she was counseled to be a source of encouragement to him in terms of his own spiritual and mental development—a role she had apparently served in their
previous experiences together. (2612-1)

A thirty-year-old man who had become extremely interested in the
Edgar Cayce information was told that in one of his past lives he had
been alive at the time of Jesus. During that lifetime he had been married
to a woman that doubted Jesus was, in fact, the long-awaited Messiah,
as she preferred instead to cling to her traditional religious upbringing.
When the man inquired if he presently knew the woman who had once
been his wife, Cayce replied in the affirmative—his wife then had returned as his mother-in-law. Interestingly enough, the woman had re-
tained her skeptical and disbelieving nature regarding the Edgar Cayce
information with which both her daughter and son-in-law had become
involved. (137-121)

A childless woman was extremely close to her nephew, a toddler. She
often had occasion to take him to the beach and frequently strangers
would stop and comment on what a beautiful child she had. She never
corrected them, allowing them to imagine that the boy was her child.
She felt unconditional love for the boy and he seemed to have the same
feelings for her in return. When the woman's brother and wife moved
out of state, taking her nephew with them, she was heartbroken. She
longed for the boy's visits, which mainly corresponded to family occasions and holidays. When asked about the past-life connection between
the two, Edgar Cayce stated that the boy had been the woman's son
during a lifetime in Palestine. Their closeness was a continuation from
that experience, and in the present their relationship was such that they
would be a "prop one to the other" throughout their lives. (1990-3)

The grandmother of a fourteen-year-old boy was told that the boy's
condition—an incoordination of the sensory system and the brain, causing the child to be unable to speak—was the result of karma. However,
it was not simply the boy's karma: Both the child and those responsible
for him were apparently meeting the memory of a previous experience
when they had been together. This joint responsibility was described as
follows: "Thus the condition is karmic in its reaction . . . for the body is

meeting itself; but so must those responsible for this entity meet themselves." (4013-1)

Later, in the course of a reading for the grandmother, this karmic connection was further clarified. It seems that the grandmother and others had once been employed in temple service in Jerusalem but had become subject to harsh edicts and strict measures governing the affairs of all individuals during the reign of Nehemiah, a ruler who helped to rebuild the walls of the city. Some individuals became so angered by Nehemiah's dictatorial control that they swore vengeance upon him. Cayce reminded the family: "And he who swears vengeance pays even unto the last farthing. So it brought developments, retardments, for when there is jealousy, hate, things that do not make the soul of man free, these bring retardments to an individual in his activities in the earth." (5177-1) On other occasions, Cayce reminded people that regardless of what other individuals had done to them hate was not an option, as there were serious karmic ramifications to hating someone else: "And the soul that holds resentment owes the soul to whom it is held, much!" (1298-1)

During a reading given to a fifty-eight-year-old grandmother, the woman inquired about her past-life connection to her grandchildren (a boy and a girl). She also wanted to know why she felt more love and concern for her grandson than she did for her granddaughter. Cayce explained that in one of her most recent incarnations her two grandchildren had been her close friends. The boy had frequently sought out her guidance and opinion, whereas the girl had been much more self-sufficient. These friendships from the past had resulted in them all being drawn back together in the present. In terms of why she felt so much more concern for one over the other, Cayce replied:

> ... there was the ability of the one to be self-sufficient—which brings an indifference; while the seeking for counsel, for help, or for instruction in the other, naturally brings the greater feeling of response. For, it is a universal and a divine law that like begets like. So, in the present experience, while there is loving—yet in the one it might be truly called loving indiffer-

> ence, while in the other it is love that is truly a creative, grow-
> ing experience in the activities of each.   1472-13

Due to the death of her brother's wife, a forty-one-year-old woman ended up with the responsibility of raising her brother's daughter—her own niece. She essentially became the girl's mother. When she asked about her connection to the child in a past-life reading from Edgar Cayce, the explanation was that she was simply picking up her relationship with the girl from an Egyptian experience when her niece had been her daughter. (2011-3)

Sometimes the karma of family relationships entails individuals incarnating back into the same family. For example, the Cayce readings state that Edgar Cayce's own grandfather eventually reincarnated into the family as Cayce's grandson. (2824-1) In a similar manner, Paula Woodruff states that a karmic connection she has with the past is with one of her own relatives. In fact, she is convinced that she and her husband are the return of her own great-grandmother and great-grandfather. The awareness came to her after her mother died and Paula inherited all of her mother's mementos and personal property. Among the belongings was an enormous chest filled with family pictures of numerous generations—people she knew as well as people she had never even seen. There were wedding pictures and portraits she hadn't known existed. One day, she was sorting through them when a friend came to visit and began looking through the pictures with her:

> My friend lifted a portrait and was taken aback by the fact that one of the older pictures looked exactly like my husband! It was a picture of my great-grandfather, whom I had never seen before. When I saw the picture, it was overwhelming! He looked exactly like my husband except for the fact that my great-grandfather appeared to have a scar on his left temple.
>
> Later, when I had the opportunity to show others the portrait, they were as amazed as my friend and I had been. There was no doubt that my husband had been my great-grandfather! As we looked through the pictures we came across a pic-

ture of a woman who was short and round, and appeared to look very much like me—the writing on the back identified the woman as my great-grandmother. I knew then and there that my husband and I had returned to the very same family.

Finally, the story of Pearl Davenport suggests that there are often connections individuals possess that may not have yet surfaced but wait until the time is right. Pearl says that her experiences have led her to believe that "we are all connected in ways that we never imagined before." One of her most memorable examples concerned a doctor that she had no conscious knowledge of. They met because, as she was being wheeled into the emergency room, "His name just rolled off my tongue and I asked for him."

After her stay in the hospital, Pearl repeatedly found herself thinking about the doctor just when he was in the midst of traumas or personal problems. Whenever he came to mind, she would call: "Whenever he needed someone, I was there—a tragedy in his life, problems with his son, the death of a close friend, a divorce, etc. I just seemed to show up exactly when he needed someone to talk to." Rather than having some kind of sexual attraction or connection, Pearl describes their relationship as follows: "I always felt responsible for him." One night she had an intense vision that made her wonder if she was going crazy:

> I was driving to work in the dark on one of the most heavily traveled roads in our area, and yet I seemed to be the only one there. When I looked up at the sky, I saw the sky turn to the color of blue velvet and the stars began to appear like diamonds. Suddenly, I saw the hands of God open up my chest and place a heart inside of me and told me to: "Keep it safe for another time." I knew that this heart belonged to my physician-friend.

The next day she contacted a talented psychic she knew to inquire what her past-life relationship had been with the doctor. The woman told her that the doctor had been her son and—without knowing of her feelings or their connection—stated that the overriding attraction was that, "You feel responsible for this man." Once the relationship was explained, Pearl no longer felt crazy; it was as if a big burden had been removed and everything began to make sense:

> What I have learned is that life is really very simple. We are all connected. Ultimately, we choose our lives and our lessons. The various lifetimes that a soul has is like the pieces of a huge quilt, all woven together—never ending, just continuing to weave its way through various experiences and relationships.

Perhaps one of the most helpful concepts contained within the Edgar Cayce files dealing with the karma of family relationships is that these experiences are purposeful for all concerned. Individuals grow through their relationships with others. To be sure, sometimes that growth can be extremely challenging but, regardless of where or with whom a person finds herself or himself; that experience is simply a lawful response to the past, enabling the individual to meet something in self in the present.

Individuals that have a strong emotional connection to one another are inevitably connected by karmic memory; however, what is done with that memory remains a matter of free will and choice. Although life's feelings, challenges and relationships are often predicated by the past, they do not predetermine the future. In fact, part of the lawfulness of karma and reincarnation is that eventually each soul will come to love all others in the same way that the Creator loves all of us—unconditionally. With this in mind, all relationships are ultimately the means through which the soul learns to love self, one another, and God, and, as Cayce once told a group of individuals studying the application of spiritual principles: "'Thou shalt love the Lord thy God with all thy heart, thy mind, thy soul; thy neighbor as thyself.' For this is the *whole* law, the *whole* law." (262-100)

6

Overcoming Personal Karma

For as ye would that men should do to you, do ye even so to them! This is not merely a rule—it is a principle, it is an active force in which one may oft see self not as through a glass darkly but as face to face with thy own ideal!   2185-1

In 1935, a thirty-three-year-old woman who had procured many readings from Edgar Cayce obtained a follow-up reading, asking for further insights into the karmic connection between herself and her two sons. Cayce reminded her that their karmic connection had already been discussed previously and suggested instead that the mother consider why souls in general (and the mother and her two sons in particular) were repeatedly drawn back together. He stated that the answer was connected to each soul's unique development as well as its destiny to become a companion to the Creator:

Hence souls in their varied experiences . . . are again and again *drawn* together by the natural law of attractive forces for the activity towards what? The *development* of the soul to the *one* purpose, the *one cause*—to be companionate with the *First Cause* *[God]!*   903-23

In other words, all relationships encountered by all people are ultimately for the growth and development of everyone involved. What this suggests is that any challenging relationship inevitably involves the need for everyone to change, grow and develop to some extent resources that the individual does not yet possess. Often the greatest barrier to personal growth may be the dynamic of wanting to make certain that the other person learns his or her lessons and meets self, rather than understanding that self is only responsible for learning one's own lessons. People can commit only to their own personal growth. People can take responsibility only for themselves. People cannot assume responsibility for someone else learning a particular lesson—they can only change themselves.

On one occasion, Edgar Cayce gave a thirty-eight-year-old businessman a definition of karma to assist the gentleman's understanding of one of the ways it could be created. The definition is connected to this very idea of learning something that the soul is presently lacking as the means of overcoming personal karma. Cayce told him: "Karma is, then, that that has been in the past builded as indifference to that known to be right! Taking chances—as it were—'[I] will do better tomorrow—this suits my purpose today—I'll do better tomorrow.'" (257-78)

Keeping this in mind, a helpful attitude in terms of overcoming personal karma is not, "I need to meet this lesson and get it over with," but is instead, "This is enabling me to become a better person . . . this will enable me to become the person I was meant to be . . . this will help me to become whole." In this manner, the purposefulness of life as well as of every relationship is made clear: to become more attuned to the soul nature of the individual and of the soul's ultimate connection to God— a connection that is the birthright of each and every soul. In regards to that purposefulness, Cayce once told a twenty-nine-year-old man: "For it is not by chance that one enters a material experience, but by the grace and mercy of an all wise universal consciousness; that each soul may become aware of its relationships to the Creative Forces, as may be manifested by and through its relationships to its fellow men." (2301-1)

Just as Cayce discussed the importance of becoming a better person through dealing with one's personal family karma, the contemporary

story of Lyn Warren details how that process can work—often in spite of
us. Through a series of life experiences, Lyn became aware of a previous
lifetime that had a tremendous impact upon her, involving a parent
from a previous incarnation returning as one of her children in the
present. Today, Lyn is an eighty-five-year-old woman who is grateful
for having had the experience as well as the challenges that it brought
to her: "I feel this experience enabled me to become free of much anger
and to learn to love. I have learned that it is possible to truly love
unconditionally . . . I still have much to learn in that area, but I've come
a long way."

Lyn remembered a past life in which she once lived as the daughter
of a domineering, controlling father, whom she had grown to hate.
Whether it was out of love, concern or temperament, her father had
attempted to hold complete dominion over her and her response had
been to become angry and rebellious. Lyn believes that a marriage,
which her father would not approve, afforded her the opportunity to
leave her father's control and she took it without hesitation, abandoning her father and their relationship in the process. All communication
between father and daughter came to an end, and Lyn never did learn
to forgive him. Her opportunity came in her present incarnation when
she found she was pregnant with her fifth child:

> Having two sons and two daughters already, I felt our family
> was well balanced and complete. One night, I was startled to
> hear an inner communication say as I was falling asleep: "It's
> time for me." Several nights later I was dropping off to sleep
> and I heard the same voice again.

Unlike Lyn's previous pregnancies, this one felt different from the
very beginning: "I knew immediately when he was conceived for he
entered with a powerful force and I started rebelling against the whole
idea of being pregnant." After he was born, Lyn found it hard to love her
new son with the same love that she shared with her previous children.
Throughout the entire experience, Lyn describes how she had become
"an angry, depressed mother." In spite of the fact that she knew better,

Lyn could not find it in her heart to love this child. Even the daily demands of having a baby in the house caused her to become angry and bitter. Almost immediately she felt as if this child held dominion over her and controlled her entire life.

Lyn describes him as being a good baby but still she resented his presence and found dealing with him a real challenge. She recalls one of her lowest points, as follows:

> One afternoon when he had awakened from his nap, he cried out just a little bit to let me know that he wanted to get up. I hurried into his room and angrily yanked him out of his crib and was rough with him as I carried him into the next room. He was only about six months old but when I came to a stop, he pushed himself away from me and looked me squarely in the eyes. I felt him ask in confusion: "What's wrong with you? I only wanted to get up?"
>
> It was then I cried out to God: "How low must I fall before you help me?"

Shortly after the experience, Lyn felt a presence in the room that she believes had come to help her. Still, the change did not come immediately: "It took me two years to love this child and it wasn't until he was six that I no longer felt that he was dominating me. In fact, when he was six I finally became the parent rather than acting the part of the rebellious child." There is no doubt in Lyn's mind that the father she had once rebelled against in her previous existence had returned in the present as her youngest son. Today, Lyn is happy to say that she loves her grown son equal to each of her other children and no longer feels the anger and resentment that had plagued her as a young mother.

It's important to note that soul growth and the overcoming of personal karma is not so much a finite goal as it is an ongoing process. Countless citations of this dynamic exist in the readings. For example, when a forty-two-year-old widow asked whether or not she and her late husband had overcome their negative karma from the past and instead grown and developed through their most recent experience with one another, Cayce replied: "The growth has been well. It will be again," (3175-1) suggesting that they had learned a great deal but that there would be more to come at some point in the future.

In another instance, a fifty-six-year-old woman who had divorced her husband wanted to know if her relationship with him had been karmic as well as whether or not she had learned her lesson. She asked: "Have I known [ex-husband] in previous lives, was the marriage a karmic debt and is it now finished?" Cayce's reply suggested that she had definitely learned specific lessons she had apparently agreed to at a soul level but their joint learning experience would continue in a subsequent lifetime together: "It is now finished. There was much to be worked out. It is complete in itself, but will be met again in another experience." (2185-1)

Although some individuals may vehemently wish to complete all of their karma with another individual in one incarnation, that desire may not always be fulfilled. As a case in point, when a thirty-five-year-old schoolteacher asked about the possibility of separating from or remaining with her husband for soul growth and development, learning the lessons that had brought the couple together, the reading advised separation. Apparently the relationship had become so negative that her staying could no longer be beneficial—the two would have to meet their karma at some point in the future. Cayce's advice was for them to "separate" and included the following rationale:

> For, where there has come those influences that make for the continued nagging, or the continued activities that become repulsive to the body-consciousness and the activities of an individual in relationships with others, this is not for the welfare or the mental associations of ideas; but the repulsiveness of body-associations and relations becomes such as to make for destructive influences in the experiences of both.   272-2

Another way of looking at this process of soul growth and meeting self is simply the fact that the lawfulness of karma eventually enables a soul to gain an awareness of what the soul is currently lacking. In other words, a lesson learned or the successful meeting of self enables the soul to move ever closer to personal wholeness and the awareness of oneness with God.

Sometimes it is challenging to understand karma when two individuals may be facing a similar experience or relationship and yet the lesson each needs to learn is very different. For example, during the course of a reading given to a twenty–year–old man who was shy and had problems in his relationships, Edgar Cayce stated that the young man needed to learn to listen and see the needs of others much more often than he spoke: "There is given only two eyes, two ears. We should hear and see twice, yes, four times as much as we say . . . " (5242-1) Conversely, a twenty–three–year–old woman also with self-esteem problems and in a karmic relationship with an overly critical father was told (in no uncertain terms) that she needed to set a spiritual ideal, become responsible for herself and learn to speak up for herself. Cayce advised: "Know thy ideal, and live to that. For, each soul must give account for its own self . . . But, so live that ye may look everyone in the face and tell him to go to hell!" (2803-2)

Obviously, in the above examples, neither individual would have been given the other person's advice. The successful meeting of self and the overcoming of personal karma involves being able to develop an awareness and a response from within the self that is currently lacking. Too often individuals mistakenly assume that karma simply entails putting up with something repeatedly, but instead the successful meeting of karmic memory more often involves coming up with new resources and new modes of behavior. The contemporary example of three grown siblings, Betty, Alan, and Nancy, provides an illustration:

As adults, the three found themselves equal owners of a family company that employed twenty–some people. According to Alan and Betty, one of their greatest challenges at work was their relationship with Nancy. As Alan tells it, "Nancy is a know–it–all. Regardless of the topic, the problem, the plan, the customer, or the employee, Nancy has the one and only answer. God forbid that Betty or I should disagree with her. Nancy is *always* right."

To be sure, Nancy has her strengths—she's adept with computers and has a thorough knowledge of the market, but the ongoing challenge of working with her for more than ten years put a strain on the siblings' relationship and on the company founded by their late father. Betty comments, as follows: "It got to the point where I didn't even want to be in the same room with her—I avoided her whenever possible, and during our weekly management meetings I generally kept my thoughts to myself, and stewed." Conversely, Alan found himself often speaking up and "flying off the handle" whenever they were together: "I couldn't begin to add up the number of times Nancy and I have argued between ourselves or in front of some of the staff." Rather than changing the situation, Alan admits all that was accomplished was Nancy's growing sense that her brother didn't like her or appreciate her contribution to the company.

Aware of the laws of reincarnation and karma, Alan said that one day, when he was "trying to figure out the karmic connection between the three of us," a possible way of solving their relationship problem finally came to him:

> I suddenly understood that I needed to quit responding to Nancy in the rash, decisive, abrupt way that can be a part of my personality. I also understood that Betty was not helping herself or the situation by remaining quiet and just becoming upset and holding everything in. I theorized that perhaps Betty and I were both supposed to be learning something from the situation and perhaps there was even something we could learn from each other. The amazing thing is that I needed to become more reflective and soft-spoken, like Betty, and it seemed that Betty needed to become more outspoken and forceful.

Although it was challenging for both Alan and Betty, they had a conversation and decided to give it a try. During their next meeting with Nancy, Betty was the one that spoke up in a more decisive manner and Alan remained reflective, although he admits he "had to say something" about one of the issues and tried to do so in a more soft-spoken manner. According to Betty, the results speak for themselves:

> Over the last six months our arguments are about one-fourth what they used to be. I can't speak for Nancy because we haven't talked about the issue in these terms, but I know Alan comes across much more calm and collected and I try to be more assertive and less of a pushover. I can't say it's always been easy. Sometimes during a meeting I see Alan's look and I know he wants to say something and doesn't or he's expecting me to say something and I haven't, but overall I think both my brother and I have grown in our capacity to deal with our sister. I also think we've grown as human beings.

In the same way that Betty and Alan came to understand that the successful meeting of karma was somehow connected to personal development and soul growth, an adult male who had ongoing problems with his father and wondered about the advisability of simply avoiding the karmic situation was counseled by Edgar Cayce:

> These conditions should be worked out in self. This should be the attitude of self . . . With what measure ye mete, with what condemnation ye make, so shall it be *measured to you again!* Ye cannot *hide* thine self in numbers, in running away to distant places or anywhere! *Self* is ever in the presence of the godly conditions of thy making . . . Ask not who will ascend to bring peace and harmony from on high, or where shall I go to seek peace and harmony abroad. *Know it must be created within thine own heart, and soul!*   1264-1

On a number of occasions, Edgar Cayce discussed the fact that growing in personal awareness and the overcoming of personal karma were inextricably connected. One example is the story of a thirty–one–year–old woman who came to him for help suffering from what was labeled "emotional hysteria." The woman's problem developed after a miscarriage and also included the loss of her voice, and the inability to swallow foods and eat normally. Although doctors thought she might have had a stroke or was suffering from a mental condition, Cayce explained that the condition was karmic and was apparently connected to the loss of a child in a former life—a condition that had been brought to her subconscious awareness after the miscarriage. He stated that she did not have a mental problem, instead the condition had arisen deep within the consciousness of her being in the form of karmic memory, resulting in the pathological condition she was experiencing. Although the treatment included various physical therapies and a specialized diet, Cayce contended that the most helpful treatment would be daily meditation, attuning to the divine within and then using that inspiration to be of "material, mental and spiritual aid to others."

What is most interesting in this case, however, is, after outlining the recommended treatment and emphasizing the importance of spiritual attunement in the woman's healing process, Cayce added that the condition could actually be reversed "almost instantly" through hypnosis. While hypnosis would not enable her to actually meet the karma and therefore should be tried only as a last resort, the condition would return or it would have to be met at some point in the woman's future. (The importance of gaining a specific awareness in this process of overcoming karma will be discussed in greater detail in the next chapter on "Karma Versus Grace.") The woman's reading ended with the following:

> For, all healing comes from the one source. And whether there is the application of foods, exercise, medicine, or even the knife—it is to bring the consciousness of the forces within the body that aid in reproducing themselves—the awareness of creative or God forces.   2696-1

Frequently, the Cayce readings demonstrate how karma can manifest through a health situation or problem because often the entire family is affected and/or involved in the problem or in the search for healing. (Refer to the story of Franklin, Julia and Debbie Wagner discussed in Chapter 3 for an earlier example). An interesting case concerned an eleven-year-old boy who came to Edgar Cayce with a severe bedwetting problem. As a last resort, the parents obtained a reading because doctors had been unable "to find a cause or cure." Regardless of what the boy ate or drank or regardless of how the boy's parents tried to help their son, the child wet the bed every single night According to the boy's mother: "Every night. We expected it. We never scolded him or blamed him, nor tried to make him unhappy over it. We tried all kinds of methods, advised by many doctors. As, no fluids after 3 o'clock, giving him salty foods and nothing to drink (supposed to absorb the fluids), etc."

During the course of the boy's reading, Cayce traced the problem to a lifetime during the late seventeenth century when he had been an associate minister and somewhat of a tyrant during the Salem witch trials. In that life the boy's name had been Marshall Whittaker, and Marshall had been fond of the practice of "ducking" a witch—plunging an individual accused of witchcraft into a lake or a pond to prove guilt or innocence. According to belief at the time, if the individual floated he or she was guilty of witchcraft; if the individual drowned he or she was innocent. The reading stated that the nightly bedwetting was essentially the lawful response for the soul's "ducking" of others; in other words, each night he was symbolically "ducking" himself. The reading went on to say that in time the bedwetting would cause an even greater emotional problem in the boy's life unless he overcame he tendency of being so condemning of others. A portion of the young man's reading is as follows:

> Before this, then, the entity was in the land of the present nativity, but during the early periods when there were those disturbances wrought by the activity of the minister of a church—as of one Marshall Whittaker.
>
> The entity then was the minister, or the associate minister, who caused the uprising and the condemnation of children who saw, who heard, who experienced the voices of those in the inter-between.
>
> And because of the entity's condemning there was brought a hardship into the experience of the entity, especially the

adopting of that rule of "ducking" others.

Hence the entity physically has experienced the ducking, from its own self, in its daily activities—which will grow to become more and more of a hindrance in self, *unless* there will be set aright that incoordination between the mental mind, or the physical mind and the spiritual mind of the individual entity, as related to condemnation of things in others.

And these, as indicated in the present, are conflicting emotions in the experience of the entity. Hence, unless changes are made, these will grow to be more and more of such a nature as to cause the entity to turn within. For, such conditions will bring that tendency for the entity to subjugate its opinions, when these become expressions, especially after the twelfth, thirteenth and fourteenth year of experience.   2779-1

To overcome the condition, as well as the soul's tendency of being condemning, the reading recommended pre–sleep suggestion. Each night as the boy was falling asleep, the parents were encouraged to make positive statements to the youth—statements that would describe the kind of behavior that the parents hoped the boy would emulate in his relationships with others. These statements were supposed to have an immediate and lasting affect upon the boy's subconscious mind. The boy's mother eventually reported on how they had followed the reading's recommendations:

At first we did nothing about it, thinking that a hypnotist was necessary, and we didn't want that. But then we thought we'd try suggestion ourselves. So I sat by his bedside and just as he was dropping off to sleep I said: "You're going to be very happy, [2779]. You're going to make many people happy. You're going to do many kind things for people. Every person you meet you will do something kind for." The very first night we tried this, *he was dry!* We kept giving him the suggestion every night and he never wet the bed again until he went to camp on the 1st of August. The counselor knew nothing about the situation; he wet the bed all the time in camp. At the end of the first week we went out to visit him, and I spoke to the Camp Counselor about it, giving him the suggestion. He gave it to [2779] every night, and he stopped wetting the bed. We continued giving the suggestion every night until the next September. Then one night we stopped, and he was dry just the same; and ever after that. The suggestion was no longer necessary. Very, very occasionally since then it has happened.

Since the successful meeting of karma often requires personal soul development, the Cayce information presents three keys to soul growth that are applicable to each and every soul. Those keys include: setting a spiritual ideal, the application of spiritual principles, and personal attunement to the divine. Each of these is discussed in greater detail below:

Setting a Spiritual Ideal

Repeatedly, the Edgar Cayce readings told individuals that the most important tool they could use to help transform their lives was to set a spiritual ideal. Essentially an ideal is a positive spiritual quality or standard that is vital in each person's movement toward wholeness. Examples might include such behaviors as unconditional love, forgiveness, empathy, oneness, cooperation, and so forth. Every spiritual ideal is essentially a component of the ultimate ideal, which is the "awareness within each soul . . . of the soul's oneness with God." (5749-14) A selection of the case histories from the Cayce files that connected the overcoming of family karma with the establishment of a spiritual ideal include the following:

When a twenty-three-year-old man asked about the means through which he could create "harmonious relations" with his mother, Cayce advised:

Set thyself a standard, an ideal. Not merely an ideal of filial or home or social relationships, or political or any other type, but

an ideal relationship as with friends and foes alike. The ideal
relationship as would be in a *mental* self to *all* associations, the
ideal relationship as in the spiritual. And know, all has to be
founded upon what spiritual ideal is. For, this alone is universal, and this alone is eternal. That which is safe, sure, peace,
harmonious, can *only* be founded on the spiritual ideal.

Know thy ideal—what it stands for! Know Who is the author of same. And then *live it!*

This will establish better relationships with self and with
the mother, with the friends and acquaintances. For, then, personalities cease to be the barriers that cause contentions or
inharmony.   1931-4

On another occasion, a woman having relationship problems with
her husband asked, "What can be done for greater harmony between
us?" The response recommended that the couple unify their purposes
and ideals:

Let each be of one purpose; not necessarily thinking the same
on questions, but their ideals and purposes. Let each think of
the other and not of self alone. Know that the relationships in
the present should be ever as much for the other as for self . . .

These each have ideals. Make them coordinate with the
material, the mental and the spiritual lives of each. Know that
it must begin in the spiritual. Then material results will be
brought into the experience as the mind is controlled towards
those ideals set by each as to the spirit with which they will
control and act in relationships one to another.   3051-4

Similarly, in a reading for a forty-four-year-old music teacher, Cayce
stated that the essential problem in the teacher's relationships with others was his tendency to be self-centered, that he had forgotten the importance of the divine in his daily life and that he had yet to set a
spiritual ideal. The reading's advice included the following:

Yet remember, "The Lord thy God is one Lord!" O that man would but attain to that consciousness and apply that principle in his dealings with every activity . . .

Thou shalt love the Lord thy God with all thy heart, thy mind, thy body: thy neighbor as thyself! . . . For this is the beginning and the end of the law . . .

Find thy ideals, and then study to show thyself approved unto same; rightly stressing the words of truth, applying them in that same phase of consciousness, whether to spiritual, mental or physical-material phases.   5142-1

Simply stated, a spiritual ideal is a motivating influence that an individual uses to measure her or his thoughts and actions. This ideal then leads to appropriate attitudes and activities that will help to manifest the spiritual ideal in daily life. As an illustration, if the chosen spiritual ideal is forgiveness then the individual would attempt to dwell upon those thoughts, attitudes and ideas that helped to nurture the ideal of forgiveness. If a parent was trying to work with the ideal of forgiveness in relationship to a grown child, for example, then any former attitudes that did not measure up to that ideal would not be appropriate. Appropriate attitudes might include such things as forgiveness itself, unconditional love, compassion, understanding, and so forth. Each of those positive attitudes should then empower activities and interactions that help to manifest that spiritual ideal. Using this same example, perhaps the attitude of forgiveness might lead to the activity of writing a note to the child in an effort to try to heal the relationship. The attitude of understanding might lead to the activity of "active listening" during the next encounter with the child. The attitude of compassion might lead to the activity of daily meditation, focusing on compassion, and so forth. It is in this manner that a spiritual ideal begins to affect and alter an individual's thoughts and activities in daily life. From Cayce's perspective, if a potential thought or action does not measure up to one's chosen spiritual ideal, then it is neither helpful nor appropriate.

When working with ideals, the readings suggested creating three columns. Label the first, "My Spiritual Ideal," and list whatever ideal is currently being worked with. Label the second, "My Mental Attitudes," and list perhaps four to seven attitudes that can best facilitate the manifestation of that spiritual ideal. Finally, label the third column, "My Physical Activities," and generate one or two activities for each of the attitudes on the list. Actually, creating an ideals chart is one of the readings' most frequent recommendations for how to apply spiritual principles in daily life.

The Application of Spiritual Principles

Once an individual has gained an awareness of specific qualities or principles that might be helpful in meeting a situation, the next step is applying those principles. For example, a thirty-six-year-old secretary who had expressed concerns about problems she was having in various karmic relationships was told: "As ye would be forgiven, so forgive in others. *That* is the manner to meet karma." (2271-1) In terms of personal application, oftentimes the readings used the phrase, "Do what you know to do and the next step will be given," suggesting that the greatest challenge in application was not so much discovering what needed to be accomplished but instead actually following through on applying it.

On another occasion, during the course of a follow-up life reading given to a thirty-three-year-old woman who wanted to know what she could do to prevent herself from becoming so upset by the "little things" that her husband did—things that apparently drove her crazy. The reading suggested that her response was simply a carryover from their English incarnation together when she had been extremely willful and disagreements between them had often been the result of her willfulness. In order to meet this karmic memory, she was told to extract herself and her will from the situation, to set it aside, and to consciously let it go. The reading assured her that in this process she could overcome her response to the situation. (2390-9) Conversely, during the husband's follow-up reading, the couple was encouraged to begin using the following affirmation each day:

Then, let the prayer of each be—three times each day—agree

upon a time—not merely say it, but feel it, be it:

"Lord! Thy will be done in me, today. Lord, thy will be done in me today."

Then, as ye go about thy daily tasks, in associations with others, let thy words, thy acts, thy thoughts, be ever, *"Lord, thy will be done in me today."*   2533-7

Similarly, Cayce encouraged a forty-four-year-old woman wanting to transform her life, overcome her personal karma and become a better person:

Practice then in thy daily experience, and thy associations with thy fellow man, charity to all, love to all; finding fault with none; being patient with all, showing brotherly love and brotherly kindness. Against these there *is* no law! And ye who have put on and as ye put on these, by the application of them in thy dealings with thy fellow man, ye become free of the laws that are of body or of mind; for ye are then conscious of being one *with* the Creative Forces that bring into the experience and consciousness of all the love of the Father for the children of men.

And it is only as ye deal with thy fellowman that ye show forth His love. For as ye do it unto the least of these, thy brethren, ye do it unto thy Maker.   1620-1

Cayce's basic advice of simply applying what one knows to do was given to a thirty-two-year-old man who apparently felt he had experienced a very karmic first marriage and subsequently a negative divorce. The man was interested in pursuing other relationships but his first marriage had left him quite fearful of getting involved with someone else. Edgar Cayce encouraged the man to simply take it one step at a time:

Then, do that thou knowest to do today! Tomorrow will be given thee the next step to take.

Be patient; be gentle; be kind. Show brotherly love. For what ye sow, ye reap. What thou art today is because of what thou hast done about that which thou didst know towards doing good.   815-3

Personal Attunement to the Divine

One of the most important transformative tools available to individuals is the act of attuning to the divine through both meditation and prayer. From Cayce's perspective, prayer and meditation were instrumental in personal development; they were also the means through which an individual could effectively cultivate his or her spiritual ideal and develop the awareness of what the soul should be about at any moment in life. The readings described prayer as talking to God and meditation as listening to the divine within. A thirty–eight–year–old man was given the following definition of each: "For prayer is supplication for direction, for understanding. Meditation is listening to the Divine within." (1861-19) The impact of personal attunement on an individual's life is described by a contemporary forty–one–year–old woman, as follows:

Before my spiritual journey began I was beaten down, angry, despondent. I didn't want to be like that but I was not able to change it—even after reading a number of self-help books. Finally, someone introduced me to meditation and it enabled me to change from within, to the very core of my being. Life is so much better, and the only thing that has really changed is me!

When a fifty–six–year–old woman came to Edgar Cayce, still holding onto regrets in her relationships, especially regrets related to a deceased sister and a karmic relationship she had once had with an old boy-friend, the reading recommended that she change her consciousness through prayer and meditation:

Open thy consciousness and let it ever be as, not merely in
words but in purposes, of hopes, of desires:

*"Here am I, o Lord, use me, send me! And may I seek only to do, to be
a channel through which thy blessings, thy promises, may be fulfilled to
my friends, my neighbors, those about me. Others, Lord, others!"*

In that attitude and in those manners may the entity fully
enter into the more perfect understanding, not seeking something from without but knowing as the body, the mind, the
soul-consciousness is attuned by meditation, by prayer to the
infinite, the voice, the feeling, the hope may all come to thee.

5276-1

Similarly, a thirty–one–year–old commercial artist interested in the
karmic connection between himself and his wife, as well as between
himself and a close friend, was informed of the connection between
soul growth and spiritual attunement:

For the law is perfect, if the entity seeks to interpret and to
apply the spiritual laws that change not except by their natural or actual growth. For each soul grows to the awareness, or
to heaven—not go to heaven but grow to heaven, that is within
the consciousness of each soul to attain if it applies self and
meets oft in the temple of the living God within the individual
entity.   3605-1

By working with these three keys to soul growth—setting a spiritual
ideal, the application of spiritual principles, and personal attunement to
the divine—individuals can overcome personal karma and grow in spiritual awareness. What follows are comments from a variety of contemporary individuals who have come to terms with the lawfulness of
karma, the dynamic and necessity of "meeting self" and the importance
of personal growth, spiritual development, and attunement to the divine:

From a forty-three-year-old man: "I have learned that all the things
that have happened to me are because of me, not society, my family, the

government, my ex-wife, or even the devil. I brought on all my problems myself. It is up to me, with God's help, to change anything that I am not happy with. We are not victims."

From a fifty-two-year-old woman: "The concepts of karma and reincarnation made me understand that you cannot 'cop out' on any life experience. It's important to learn to roll with every punch, or every challenge that comes your way, and ultimately we need to learn how to love ourselves and one another unconditionally."

A fifty-nine-year-old woman states: "I have overcome my long-lasting inferiority complexes and my fears of doing innovative, challenging tasks. I have learned to take responsibility for my mistakes and to go on searching to better myself."

A sixty-two-year-old man attributes his ability to comprehend life's lessons and his individual purpose to his awareness of the laws of reincarnation and karma: "For me, understanding how life works in terms of reincarnation and karma have been extremely helpful in understanding such questions as: 'Who am I?' 'Why am I here?' 'Where am I going?' and 'What is the purpose of life?'"

A forty-six-year-old man has a similar response:

> Knowing about my past lives helped me to work on letting go of unconscious resentment and anger. It also helped me to understand why I so often felt on guard around my father. I worked on learning that he really didn't owe me anything. I worked on forgiveness and letting go of the idea that something was owed me. It really helped me to understand that my father didn't owe me anything.

A fifty-two-year-old woman adds: "Understanding karma has been extremely helpful in explaining my loves and hates, my fears and phobias, particularly those involving people who are close to me. In addition, approaching things—even bad things—with love has made a profound difference on my life."

Another woman offers the following: "We contract for learning in our various lives, trying to apply the best that we know. Sooner or later we will all make it. Ultimately, we help each other along the way. I get exactly what I need, when I need it. There are no victims in the universe."

A woman in her fifties discusses how a seemingly difficult challenge ended up being for her own good: "My divorce resulted in great growth for me. I feel I became a much stronger person and a much greater artist. I published a book on creativity and personal growth, became well known as an artist, got my MA, developed a business, began teaching on a university level, and so on."

A seventy-four-year-old woman had this to say: "It took me years to realize how loved I am. For so long I felt so invisible and insignificant. I tried so hard to be perfect and worthy. Now, I finally realize that I am a channel of blessings, and I try to reflect to others the bountiful love of God that so fills my heart. My cup runneth over and can't hold it in. I am so blessed."

A parent of three grown children learned the following:

> I have come to know that my children are not an extension of myself but individuals on their own separate paths. We have come together for a joint purpose but their paths are uniquely their own. Perhaps I can be a role model for them and teach them and equally learn from them but I cannot know their path or purpose, I can only strive to find my own.

Because of his life experiences and his growing awareness, a fifty-year-old man now understands the ongoing nature of soul growth: "I am far from being a perfect person but I have become a much better person. I have gotten to the point where I generally ask myself, 'What am I supposed to be learning from this?' Ultimately, all of my relationships have helped me to become a better person."

Finally, a middle-aged woman recites all she has learned in this ongoing process of overcoming her personal karma:

> I've learned patience and compassion through caring for parents and grandparents that were ill.

I've learned that life will bring me what I need and that worry is an unnecessary habit. Numerous times what I've needed has fallen right into my lap with such uncanny timing that it goes far beyond coincidence.

I've learned that only brutal honesty when examining the self will yield worthwhile results. When it comes to personal growth, the ego—with all of its built in defense mechanisms—has to be set aside.

I've learned that other people really are my magic mirror and I study them and my feelings towards them in order to better understand myself. For example, I've learned to be more sensitive to others when I speak. This came from working with someone who was so incredibly insensitive that I would cringe from the things she would say to others or myself. After years of being exposed to this I found myself hearing her voice in my head when I said something even remotely insensitive or negative. It was quite a deterrent and although it was unpleasant I am grateful for the growth that it brought me.

Overcoming personal karma inevitably entails a growth in personal awareness. It is this growth that enables the individual to lawfully meet a karmic memory and to acquire personal resources that were perhaps lacking in the soul's movement toward wholeness. This growth toward wholeness is often achieved through dealing with and overcoming personal challenges and in working through the difficulties of karmic relationships. It is a process in which every individual is involved, an ongoing process of growth and enlightenment. It is a process in which every individual will eventually come to understand the nature of the soul, the connection each soul has with one another and the unfathomable relationship each soul ultimately possesses with the Creator.

7

Karma Versus Grace

Thus we may through those administrations of that which is the spirit of truth made manifest, turn this karma, or law, to grace and mercy.   5209-1

Upon hearing the terms "karma" and "grace," some individuals may not at first see any connection between the two but both are laws that operate within the absolute lawfulness of the universe. Both are also inextricably connected to each soul's movement toward wholeness. An essential difference between the two, however, is that the law of grace empowers an individual with the divine pattern of the Creator in the process of meeting self, whereas the law of karma leaves the self with self's resources alone.

On one occasion, while describing how meeting self could be accomplished through either karma or grace, Cayce told a thirty-two-year-old sheet metal worker:

> For the law of the Lord is perfect, and whatsoever an entity, an individual sows, that must he reap . . . As to whether one meets it in the letter of the law or in mercy, in grace, becomes

the choice of the entity. If one would have mercy, grace, love, friends, one must show self in such a manner to those with whom one becomes associated. For like begets like.   5001-1

The New Testament tells us that the law of karma is superceded by the law of grace when discussing the fruits of the spirit: "But the fruit of the Spirit is love, joy, peace, longsuffering, gentleness, goodness, faith, meekness, temperance: *against such there is no law.*" (Galatians 5:22–23; emphasis mine) Each of these fruits of the spirit are essentially components of a consciousness described as the universal Christ Consciousness: "the awareness within each soul, imprinted in pattern on the mind and waiting to be awakened by the will, of the soul's oneness with God." (5749-14)

The Cayce readings state that this consciousness was perfectly manifested by Jesus. However, rather than thinking that this awareness is somehow connected to the religion of Christianity (after all, Jesus was not a Christian, He was a Jew), it is important to realize that it instead depends on the perfect manifestation of the fruits of the spirit by any individual. In other words, Christ Consciousness is the birthright of each and every soul, regardless of his or her religion.

What may be conceptually challenging to some people is the idea that living a life in accord with the spirit is not necessarily a matter of religion. But Jesus Himself stated that His mission was not really to change religion nor was it to somehow put the religion of the Old Testament prophets back on track. Instead, it was to perfectly manifest the laws of the Creator in the earth and in the process fulfill the meeting of self:

Think not that I come to destroy the law, or the prophets: I am not come to destroy, but to fulfill.

For verily I say unto you, till heaven and earth pass, one jot or one tittle shall in no wise pass from the law, till all be fulfilled.   (Matthew 5:17-18)

Regardless of whether an individual becomes subject to karma alone or is empowered with grace, the lawfulness of life does not change—he or she must still eventually meet self. Grace does not do away with the necessity of meeting self; it enables the individual to meet self in the best possible manner by putting self in accord with the pattern of spiritual perfection that was demonstrated by Jesus. In this process, the soul avails itself of the grace of God.

An example from the Cayce files is the case of a fifty-two-year-old schoolteacher who asked for guidance and direction in order to deal with her personal karma. Cayce explained that karma could best be met by aligning self with the pattern of the Christ Consciousness, as demonstrated by Jesus: "Not that every soul shall not give account for the deeds done in body, and in the body meet them! But in each meeting, in *each* activity, let the pattern [of the Christ Consciousness]—not in self, not in mind alone, but in Him—be the guide." (2067-2) In the same reading, the woman was told that by putting her life in perfect accord with the pattern of Christ's life, she would eventually transform all of her karma: "He *alone* is each soul pattern! *He* is thy *karma*, if ye put thy trust *wholly* in Him!"

Rather than seeing the soul pattern of Jesus as being *allegiance to* a particular faith, it would be more accurate to see it as *conformity with* divine spirit and the resulting behavior. Cayce went on to describe this pattern as "doing good, being kind, being patient, being loving in *every* experience of man's activity." Another way of understanding the helpfulness of the pattern set by Jesus is to realize that, regardless of what issues or experiences an individual may be facing in the present, those issues have already been met by Jesus as He lived in perfect accord with the laws of the Creator.

Cayce author and scholar Lynn Sparrow once described Jesus' life as a map that could be followed through the oftentimes-confusing issues in the maze of life:

> Perhaps we can best understand the compatibility of karma and grace by looking at an analogy. Suppose you are in the center of a maze, and your job is to get out. Now there are two ways that you can go about getting through the maze. You can

blindly fumble and bumble your way down various corridors. When you hit a dead end, you must go back and retrace your steps to the point where you made the wrong turn, then try once again . . . This path of trial and error would be like taking the way of karma . . .

Suppose, on the other hand, that someone said to you, "I've successfully completed that maze, and I have a map that shows every turn. Furthermore, if you'll accept my map, I'll impart to you the strength and wisdom you need to follow my map. You may not understand how I can give you this special help, but if you will just accept it, you will experience it working on your trip through the maze. You will succeed, not through your own efforts, but by trusting that I have already secured your release from this maze." This would be the way of grace: accepting the map—which would be analogous to Jesus as the pattern—and accepting the power to follow the map.

(Sparrow, pg. 202)

Along the same lines, Edgar Cayce told a fifty-seven-year-old man interested in healing the karma he had with his immediate family that the best approach was to live in accord with the pattern of the Christ Consciousness that had been exemplified by Jesus: "For, since the foundations of the world He has paved the ways, here and there entering into the experience of man's existence that He may know every temptation that might beset man in all of his ways." (442-3)

In 1933, an individual who had obtained readings for both himself and his mother wrote a letter to Edgar Cayce and inquired about what the readings had to say regarding karmic influences. Cayce's reply suggested that the law of karma could be wiped away with the law of grace by living in accord with the soul's pattern of perfection and becoming "godlike in the world." A portion of Cayce's response to Mr. [256] follows:

Yes, the readings have had a great deal to say about Karmic influences, and that—according to the readings—is where the saving grace of the Christ comes in our activity . . .

Yes, the [karmic] obligations that individuals have one to another from former associations must be met. This accounts for the attraction individuals have, or the repellent forces that come. Of course, realizing this in relationship to individuals, and as to what is the saving grace or power with such associations wherever karmic influences must be worked out, or where obligations are due, we know that the ministrations in the manner of the Christ's injunctions may wipe out any bill—we might say—in the opposite direction . . . Man alone is given a soul, with the power to be a co-creator with God, having the ability—through his will—to separate himself from the divine forces or powers. This is determined by his associations with his fellow man, who—as himself—is a manifestation, with the ability to become godlike in his associations with the whole, or with all forms of life as manifested in the Christ Consciousness or the Christ Life; for He became the Son to whom all power was given in heaven and in earth, in exchange for His ability to manifest God's force, God's power, or to become *godlike* in the world; thus, He became the Savior of men, through His ability to manifest life in its correct relationship and form in the earth. Hence man may turn to Him for whatever may be necessary for him to make right with this fellow man, through the counsel, through the love He manifested. We each arrive at that position at some time, or every day in our experience, when we have to answer the question "What will ye do with this man called Jesus?"   256-1 Report File

One component of the "letter of the law" that governs karmic memory has to do with the *quantitative* response an individual encounters in the process of meeting self. In other words, part of the lawfulness of "what you sow you must reap" is that an individual meets karmic memory in equal measure to how that memory was created. If a person did something out of accord with the pattern of wholeness "X" number of times to someone else, then he or she would have to personally encounter the same situation in life the same number of times in order to meet it.

Grace, however, has the ability to do away with the quantity and instead enables the individual to meet the situation and gain the necessary awareness with a *qualitative* response. This is essentially meeting self in the spirit of the law rather than the letter of the law.

When a group of individuals in New York requested a reading from Edgar Cayce on the possibility of understanding karma and studying, researching and proving the topic of reincarnation, Cayce suggested that the life of King David in the Old Testament would be a helpful pattern for them to study:

> Using the experience of David the king as an example, what was it in his experience that caused him to be called a man after God's own heart? That he did not falter, that he did not do this or that or be guilty of every immoral experience in the category of man's relationship? Rather was it that he was sorry, and not guilty of the same offence twice!
>
> Well that ye pattern thy study of thyself after such a life!
>
> 5753-2

The same reading also explained the proper rationale for studying the topics of reincarnation and karma in the first place:

> And to find that ye only lived, died and were buried under the cherry tree in Grandmother's garden does not make thee one whit better neighbor, citizen, mother or father!
>
> But to know that ye spoke unkindly and suffered for it, and in the present may correct it by being righteous—*that* is worth while!
>
> What is righteousness? Just being kind, just being noble, just being self-sacrificing; just being willing to be the hands for the blind, the feet for the lame—these are constructive experiences.
>
> Ye may gain knowledge of same, for incarnations *are* a *fact!*
>
> How may ye prove it? In thy daily living!

As individuals attune themselves to the soul's pattern of wholeness, not only is the individual better able to meet self but all of the memories of past experiences may be brought to the soul's awareness in the process. This is referred to in the New Testament when Jesus speaks about "the Comforter" (the Holy Spirit): " . . . he shall teach you all things, and bring all things to your remembrance, whatsoever I have said unto you." (John 14:26) A fascinating account of how this bringing of "all things to your remembrance" might be experienced is told by Blanche Nelson, who had the following experience:

> One morning, as I awoke, I became aware of a man standing beside my bed. I had the impression of white hair and a beard and he was wearing a white robe as well. He was a being of light and was bent over me with his arm outstretched and his hand positioned above my forehead. He said the word, "Remember!" He repeated this word and he said it with such intensity and focus that my mind followed his command . . .
>
> I was amazed at what I knew. The structure of the universe, the mystery of all creation, the purpose of not only my own life, but also the lives of everyone I knew. From the forming of atoms to the complexities of the soul, from human development to the millions of other life forms in all of creation, from the stars in the physical world to the memory of every detail of every life I have ever lived, all these things and much, much more, were known to me. Knowledge that would have taken hundreds of years to learn on earth was now a part of me.
>
> I stood upon a precipice overlooking the universe, reveling in this knowledge, filled with an indescribable peace. I remember thinking, "But it's so simple! Why a child could understand it! How could it be that I have been living so long and never saw this while I was in the body!? It's so perfect! And so obvious!"
>
> Suddenly something monumental I had understood was gone! It was like having something on the tip of your tongue, just beyond your ability to bring it forth, this was how I felt,

but this wasn't just some name of a movie or of a phone number, this was a HUGE loss. I tried to focus on it and recall it and as I did so, another large chunk of knowledge disappeared. And so a snowball effect began and the harder I tried to retain this precious gift, the faster it began to slip from my grasp. I began falling back and soon found myself back in my body with my spiritual traveler standing over me saying, "Remember . . . remember!"

All I remember is what I've written here.

Elizabeth Reynolds was fifty-seven years old when she obtained a reading from Edgar Cayce. One of her greatest karmic challenges was her husband, from whom she was separated. In addition to wanting to know where the karma with her husband had originated, Elizabeth was apparently wondering whether their getting together had been a mistake; Cayce assured her that it had not: "As has been indicated through these channels, there is never a chance meeting, or any association, that hasn't its meaning or purpose in the development of an individual entity or soul." (1648-2) The karma that she was facing was traced to a lifetimes the couple had been together as brother and sister.

In terms of how she could best meet karmic memory in the present, the reading told Elizabeth that if an individual focused on self alone, she or he would remain subject to karma, whereas by focusing on the soul's pattern of wholeness the person would open to grace, the karma would be met, and the individual would move toward greater soul development.

A thirty-six-year-old insurance agent was given similar advice:

For, it is not by chance that each entity enters, but that the entity—as a part of the whole—may fill that place which no other soul may fill so well. For He hath not willed that any soul should perish. Thus with each material manifestation there is an undertaking by an entity to so manifest that it, as a part of the whole, may become more and more attuned to that consciousness, and thus glorify Him in the entity's relationships to others in any and in every experience.

Each soul was, is, and is to be a companion with that creative influence or force called God. Thus each entity is a child
of God, or is a part of that whole.   2533-1

The Cayce material states that the purpose of life is to move ever
closer toward personal wholeness and the soul's awareness of its ultimate relationship to God. Two laws that assist all individuals in this
process are the laws of karma and grace. The law of karma enables an
individual to meet memory patterns within the self that are out of harmony with the soul's oneness with the Creator. Meeting these karmic
memory patterns enables an individual to grow in awareness through
personal challenges and obedience to the law. Grace provides a means
to gain the necessary awareness without having to necessarily meet the
same measure of karmic memory created. Regardless of whether an
individual chooses to remain subject to the law of karma or instead
align with the pattern of the law of grace, the lawfulness of the universe
does not change.

Conclusion

Thus we may through those administrations of that which is the spirit of truth made manifest, turn this karma, or law, to grace and mercy.   5209-1

Families are purposeful, and every person in one's family is there for a reason. Ultimately, that reason is to enable all individuals to grow in soul development and personal wholeness, becoming better people in the process. Along the way each individual meets self, healing karmic memory patterns that are of harmony with the soul's awareness of its connection to the rest of Creation and its oneness with the Creator. Each relationship experienced by all individuals has the capacity to bring a person ever closer to an awareness of that oneness. Even the most difficult of family relationships can be viewed as an individual's soul choice, leading to personal growth. As Edgar Cayce told one woman, "then in *every* contact is there the opportunity for an entity, a soul, to fulfil or meet itself . . . " (903-23) With this in mind, there is an underlying purposefulness behind every relationship and each experience a soul encounters.

In the process of compiling information for the "Philosophy" chapter of Cayce's biography, *There Is a River*, author Thomas Sugrue wanted to know if souls generally made progress in their experiences in the earth with the following question: "Is the average fulfillment of the soul's expectation [of lessons to be learned] more or less than fifty percent?" Cayce's answer suggests that in spite of how things may sometimes appear in the outer world there is growth. He replied, "It's a continuous advancement, so it is more than fifty percent." (5749-14) Cayce went on to say that an understanding of the laws of reincarnation and karma had once been an integral part of Christianity but they had been removed by founders of the early Church in "the attempts to take short cuts."

Oftentimes, the readings explained the lawfulness of karma by stating that whatever an individual sowed would eventually have to be reaped. Although some individuals might use this cause–and–effect dynamic to describe karma as justice, a consequence or even a debt, it is most accurate to describe it as a pool of unconscious memory. To be sure, an individual draws upon karmic memory in a variety of ways in her or his present experience, but karma is simply memory. This memory has elements that may appear to be both positive and negative. For example, a lifelong closeness to one family member is as likely to be karmic as an ongoing animosity to another. Although karma definitely has an effect upon life and one's attitude toward others, the exercise of free will determines the actual experience an individual has in the present.

In practical terms, individuals may not always be able to understand why a certain relationship was drawn to them, but the "why" may not be primary. What is important is "how" individuals choose to respond to each relationship and life experience. Imagine, for example, that two people encounter a similar circumstance in their upbringing—perhaps an overly critical parent—yet each person chooses to deal with the situation in a very different manner. One might spend a lifetime remaining angry and bitter, perhaps becoming overly critical in response, and the other might instead work through the situation by forgiving the parent and vowing to never exhibit similar traits in his or her relationships with others. Although the situation starts out the same, each person's choice determines a very different life experience.

Sometimes an understanding of karmic connections can be conceptually challenging in that there really isn't karma *between* people; instead, memory exists in *relationship to* people and is really a karmic experience within one's self. However, people come to terms with that memory or meet themselves most effectively through interaction with others. This interesting dynamic of family relationships can mislead people to perceive various family members as the source of their challenges and frustrations, rather than accepting personal responsibility.

The Cayce readings indicate that each individual retains the memory of former experiences, often as patterns that manifest through the emotional and even cellular levels of the body. These memory patterns must be met and their "meeting" generally entails a growth in personal awareness. In this manner an individual lawfully meets personal karma and acquires personal resources and growth in awareness that are necessary for the soul's personal development.

In this process of growing toward at-one-ment with the Creator, there is a choice: An individual can repeatedly meet his or her own karmic memory and allow it to remain a stumblingblock in life, or the individual can open to the law of grace and draw upon the pattern of wholeness inherent in every situation. In this manner, personal karma and life's challenges can instead become stepping-stones toward greater development.

Individuals avail themselves of grace by putting themselves in accord with the fruits of the spirit, by aligning to the soul's pattern of wholeness and perfection and by consciously choosing a path of personal growth and development. From the perspective of the Cayce readings, three tools that are extremely effective in soul growth entail the setting of spiritual ideals, the application of spiritual principles in everyday life and becoming personally attuned to the divine.

Family karma is not some kind of punishment or divine retribution; instead, it is the means through which individuals can gain an awareness of themselves, their relationships to all others and ultimately their relationship to the Creator. Family karma is the lawful response to choices and actions that have occurred in the past. It demonstrates the exacting nature of individual responsibility and it allows for the ever-present hopefulness of personal free will. In the end, family karma enables every individual to have the opportunity to become a better person for having had the experience of being in that family. It also enables each individual to eventually come to the realization that the Creator is all loving and fair, and that life is now and will forever be a completely lawful experience.

Notes

1. For a more thorough examination of reincarnation and karma in the Bible, see *Why Jesus Taught Reincarnation* by Herbert Bruce Puryear, Ph.D.

2. In addition to *There Is a River*, by Thomas Sugrue, a further examination of Cayce's life and work can be found in Sidney D. Kirkpatrick's *Edgar Cayce: An American Prophet*.

3. The Edgar Cayce readings are numbered to maintain confidentiality. The first set of numbers (e.g. "440") refers to the individual or group for whom the reading was given. The second set of numbers (e.g. "5") refers to the number of the reading for that individual or group.

4. For the most part, all names used within this volume have been changed to maintain confidentiality.

5. "Candid Camera of the Cosmos," by Gina Cerminara. *A.R.E. Bulletin*, November 1945.

6. For additional information on the topic of soul mates, see *Edgar Cayce on Soul Mates* by Kevin J. Todeschi.

References and Recommended Reading

Bowman, Carol. *Children's Past Lives: How Past Life Memories Affect Your Child.* New York: Bantam, 1998.

Cerminara, Gina. *Many Mansions.* New York: New American Library, 1967.

Easton, Stewart C., translator. *Man and the World in the Light of Anthroposophy.* Spring Valley, New York: Anthroposophic Press, 1975.

Hamilton, Edith. *Mythology.* Boston: Back Bay Books (Little Brown and Company), 1998.

The Holy Bible, King James Version, 1979.

Puryear, Herbert Bruce, Ph.D. *Why Jesus Taught Reincarnation: A Better News Gospel.* Scottsdale, Arizona: New Paradigm Press, 1992.

Smith, Huston. *The World's Religions.* New York: HarperCollins, 1991.

Sparrow, Lynn Elwell. *Edgar Cayce and Christian Faith.* Virginia Beach, Virginia: A.R.E. Press, 1999.

Stevenson, Ian. *Twenty Cases Suggestive of Reincarnation.* Charlottesville, Virginia: University Press of Virginia, 1974.

Sugrue, Thomas. *There Is a River.* Virginia Beach, Virginia: A.R.E. Press, 1997.

Todeschi, Kevin J. *Edgar Cayce on the Akashic Records.* Virginia Beach, Virginia: A.R.E. Press, 1998.

Todeschi, Kevin J. *Edgar Cayce on Soul Mates.* Virginia Beach, Virginia: A.R.E. Press, 1999.

Weiss, Brian. *Only Love Is Real: A Story of Soulmates Reunited.* New York: Warner Books, 1996.

A.R.E. PRESS

The A.R.E. Press publishes books, videos, and audiotapes meant to improve the quality of our readers' lives—personally, professionally, and spiritually. We hope our products support your endeavors to realize your career potential, to enhance your relationships, to improve your health, and to encourage you to make the changes necessary to live a loving, joyful, and fulfilling life.

For more information or to receive a free catalog, call:

1-800-723-1112

Or write:

A.R.E. Press
215 67th Street
Virginia Beach, VA 23451-2061